# CAREER DIARY™

## OF AN

## ANIMATION

## PRODUCER

Thirty days behind the scenes
with a professional.

GARDNER'S GUIDE® SERIES

*SUE RIEDL*

GARTH GARDNER COMPANY

*GGC publishing*

Washington DC, USA · London, UK

Art Director: Nic Banks
Editor: Natarsha Bryant
Photographs: Author
Project Director: Garth Gardner

Editorial inquiries concerning this book should be e-mailed to:
info@ggcinc.com
www.gogardner.com

Library of Congress Cataloging-in-Publication Data

Riedl, Sue.
  Career diary of an animation producer / Sue Riedl.
      p. cm. -- (Gardner's guide series)
    ISBN 1-58965-011-5
  1. Animation (Cinematography)--Vocational guidance. I. Title. II.
Series.
    TR897.5.R54 2003
    791.43'3--dc21
                                         2003004895

# TABLE OF CONTENTS

5 Introduction: Author's Biography

13 Resumé

19 Day 1

29 Day 2

34 Day 3

39 Day 4

42 Day 5

46 Day 6

51 Day 7

55 Day 8

60 Day 9

65 Day 10

71 Day 11

77 Day 12

83 Day 13

89 Day 14

94 Day 15

98 Day 16

102 Day 17

106 Day 18

109 Day 19

112 Day 20

115 Day 21

119 Day 22

123 Day 23

128 Day 24

131 Day 25

135 Day 26

138 Day 27

141 Day 28

146 Day 29

152 Day 30

# BIOGRAPHY

How did I get into producing?

Hmmm, I never really intended to be a producer. When I left school, I graduated with a BAH (Bachelor's of Arts) in Film Studies from Queen's University in Kingston, Ontario (that's in Canada!). I was at the same spot every graduate is, unless she is pretty lucky, I had no idea how to get a job in the film industry. I had nothing to put on my resume, no idea who to call-or worse, I didn't know how to even get someone to take my call! I got my first job through a friend, which it was really a lucky break. She had graduated a year before me and had become an assistant editor at a commercial film company called Partners. She was moving on to edit a TV series and suggested me as her replacement. Of course, I took the job, but how or why the editor of the series (Lorenzo) agreed to hire me, I don't know.

I knew nothing! I didn't even know what non-linear editing was or even seen an AVID. I had cut my short films on a flatbed. I spent hours reading the AVID manual, barely understanding a word and long nights learning the software. Thankfully, I had many really amazing and supportive co-workers who helped me get started. I learned a lot about post-production, commercial work, dealing with clients and was formally introduced to the industry.

I was at Partners for about a year when I was offered a project coordinator job at a post-production company called Mag North. I was referred for this particular position through a friend I had worked with at Partners who had moved on to manage Mag North's client service department. Actually, I think that every job I have ever had was through a contact or friend in the industry. I guess you don't always need a resume to get a job. Anyway, Mag North does mainly series work-transfers/dailies, edits and final colour corrections. I learned a lot about how a film goes through post-production and how to deliver a final master. I left there after about a year. Just when I said that I needed a change, I got a call from Lorenzo, the editor I had worked with at Partners. He was editing a docu/drama about Alien life and needed an assistant. I took the job even though it was only a 2-month contract.

Working with Lorenzo on "Aliens: Are We Alone" was an interesting experience. I had to work nights, since Lorenzo cut during the day. Immediately, I learned to solve many of my own technical problems, since no one was around. I loathe working with tape decks, patching cables, and all that, it was a good experience.

I needed a break when that show ended, but I also was worried. It was June. I didn't have a lot of money saved and really didn't know what I wanted to do. Perhaps, I should explore being a post-production coordinator. No such luck, I couldn't uncover any opportunities and I needed a job.

September, I was panicking. What the earth was I going to do? My friend Paula called to tell me that GVFX (a visual effects company) was looking for a coordinator. I didn't immediately make the call; after all, I knew nothing about visual effects. By desperation time(mid-September), I put in the call. I interviewed with GVFX and got the job. I was there about 8 months and doing pretty well. It was a bit grueling, and had long hours, but the visual effects stuff was interesting and the people were great. This was another huge learning experience.

I left when I was accepted into the Canadian Film Centre Director's program. (Did I mention that I really want to direct? Well, it's true, me and everyone else). School was great, but, I was broke when I got out of school and I needed a job fast.

GVFX asked me to come back, and I took a job as a Digital Effects Producer in the VFX department. I scheduled all the shots going through the shop, worked with the Visual Effects Supervisors and made sure we delivered our shows on time. I also budgeted and quoted on shows that came through the post-department, sometimes with a supervisor and sometimes on my own. I had become friends with Jon, one of the FX Supervisors and decided I'd rather be an FX Assistant. This means working on one show and being involved in pre-production, shooting (supervising VFX on set to make sure all the plates are right and getting proper measurements for 3D) and then following through to post. Therefore, I quit my other job and suddenly, was out of work for 5 months! The show I was supposed to go directly on with Jon was put on hold. In fact, it never happened.

I didn't work again until a Hallmark Show called "Prince Charming" started late that summer. I worked on that until the next Spring (May). It was filled with challenging and difficult long hours. Most of all, I knew I didn't want to work in Visual Effects anymore. I wanted to work a job that I found creative and fulfilling and had regular hours. I wanted a life.

I have always loved stop-motion animation and so I thought, maybe I should try to get a job at a stop-motion company. A friend of mine mentioned a place called Head Gear Animation. I didn't know what position I could apply for, but I put together my resume, a reel of some of my stop-motion films (yep, I've made my small attempt at animation), and decided to go by. After about an hour of standing outside, I even walked in. I was really that nervous! I was there about 10 minutes, long enough to drop off my stuff and leave in horror. I realized that my films looked like kid's work compared to what they did. Maybe I'd be lucky and they'd lose my tape...that was in May 2001.

September 2001. Still no job. One morning when I had run out of anyone to call, fax, or ask for work, I decided to email people I even remotely knew in the business. Half an hour later I got an email back from the owner of an "FX" company called Mr.X. He heard that the company down the hall, Head Gear Animation, was looking for a producer(how weird is that?). I called and Paula answered. They were interviewing people. I went in for the interview. A few weeks later, I was offered the job.

Before I knew it, I was running out of space. However, I must admit, I was really in LOVE with this job! Working there was amazing! Everyone was so talented and great to work with. I even left at a reasonable hour on a daily basis!

I almost forgot to mention that I have producing experience from my own directing ambitions (I wasn't kidding!). I have produced four of my own shorts and worked on many others. Currently, I am working on developing a feature film with a producer and writer (I'm just the director on this one) and have a TV series in development with my writing partner Mary. Being in the independent film world forces you to know a lot of details about the entire production and post process.

...And that is my story. I feel that I am the luckiest person in the world and in many ways, I guess I am!

## CURRENT POSITIONS AND RESPONSIBILITIES

Producer-Head Gear Animation

Head Gear Animation is a small company owned by Steve Angel and Julian Grey. We do stop-motion animation, cel and mixed media. We also occasionally do live shoots. There are six core employees-four director/animators-Julian, Steve, Drew and Isaac. Then there's Paula who is the marketing director and myself, the producer. Quite often, we have a couple post-production people working with us-usually Kyle, Nick or Jason. We do commercial work and broadcast design. Head Gear's work has won numerous awards for spots ranging from Sesame Street to a commercial for IKEA.

My job starts when we're asked to bid on a project. I'm always the contact person for the client and the liaison between their creative team and ours. I start by getting all the information we need to bid on the job-length, storyboards, animation style, etc. I then put together a bid. Steve, Julian and I always settle on a final number; but I'll usually present a budget to them independently-as a starting point. Usually, we go back and forth before agreeing on a number. Often times, I need to defend our budget or decide if we can bring the price down. Then, hopefully the job is awarded to us.

Once that happens, I put together a schedule with delivery dates, client and agency screenings and any other approval deadlines. I figure out who'll work on the project and if we need to hire anyone else. When we need freelancers, I discuss the work period and rate with them before they're hired. Finally, I book any production or post sessions /equipment we'll need to complete the job. I send the schedule to the client and make sure we stick to it.

During the production process, my job is to deal with any issues that arise-internally or with the client. We always like to have conference calls with all of the creative teams to discuss any differences of opinion-but if there is disagreement, I am there to act as a barrier between the directors and the client so that the creative process remains as hassle free as possible.

Each job is different and each requires different last minute planning, extra help, schedule juggling, etc. I'm there to deal with all that stuff. At Head Gear I also get the drinks and snacks for client meetings, answer the phone, handle payroll (when needed), and I'll do the dishes when they've piled up. It can be stressful but overall it's a lot of fun and always inspiring to see the work that comes out of this company.

# RÉSUMÉ

## EMPLOYMENT

### PRODUCER, HEAD GEAR ANIMATION
### 2001-PRESENT

Produced various stop-motion commercials including spots for IKEA, Jolly Rancher, Crystal Light, Turtles and YTV and The Cartoon Network

### VISUAL EFFECTS ASSISTANT 2001

Prince Charming - Hallmark/ TNT

### VISUAL EFFECTS PRODUCER (WITH GVFX)
### 1997-2000

Thomas and The Magic Railroad - Britt Allcroft Productions

Bride of Chucky - Universal

Shot Through the Heart - Alliance

The Great Gatsby (1999) - A&E

The Crossing - A&E

Relic Hunter Season 1 - Fireworks Entertainment

A Touch of Hope - NBC Television

Twice in a Lifetime - PAX Television

Stargate SG-1 - MGM Television

ICE - ABC / Alexander Enright

## ASSISTANT EDITOR, CINENOVA PRODUCTIONS, "ALIENS ARE WE ALONE", SPRING 1997

## POST PRODUCTION COORDINATOR, MAGNETIC NORTH 1996-1997

Coordinated TV series. TV movies and feature films through transfer to final master within the post -facility

## ASSISTANT EDITOR, PARTNERS FILM COMPANY, 1995-1996

## TRAINING/ EDUCATION

Canadian Film Centre
Director Residency Programme 1998

Queen's University, BAH, Film 1994

**Acting 110-Introduction to Acting – Queen's University 1993

# FILMOGRAPHY - DIRECTOR

**NEAR DEATH**, 90 minutes, 35mm feature film

A satiric black comedy about a woman searching for the meaning of life by turning to murder. In development through the National Screen Institute/Telefilm Features First Development Program.

**HEAD STICK'EM**, 5 minutes, 16mm animated

Short (stop-motion) about a woman can't keep her head on. 2001

Nominated for Best Animation at the Yorkton Short Film Festival 2002

**SALAMI HEAVEN**, 10 minutes, 8mm live action and 16mm animation.

A woman's life is overwhelmed with salami. 2000

· Nominated for Best Comedy, Best Script and Best Editing at the Yorkton Short Film Festival

· Second prize for BEST ANIMATION at the Canadian International Film and Video Festival

· Best Animation and Runner Up People's Choice Award-Cabbagetown Film Festival

· Screened at The Montreal Film Festival, Victoria Film Festival, St. John's Women's Film Festival, the Women

Make Waves Festival in Taiwan and the San Paolo Festival in Brazil.

*DINNER: THE MUSICAL*, 17 minutes, BETA SP.

Comedic film about a couple trying to re-ignite their passion- completed for the Canadian Film Centre's Director's Program. 1998

*SLIGHTLY PARANOID*, A short film about a strange smell. 1996

· Screened at various festivals including-Montreal World Film Festival, Images Film Festival and the Canadian Int'l Film and Video Festival.

· Purchased for broadcast by CBC "Reflections" and WTN

*MAKEOVER*, 8 minute, 16mm animated comedic short about women and body image. 1994

Packaged for educational programming for use in high school and university health programs.

## WRITING

*TALLULAH BIGHEAD: GIRL GUMSHOE*, An animated children's series about a little girl detective with an oversize head.

(Co-created with Mary MacNaughton)

Optioned in 2002 to Joan Lambur and Associates-in development with YTV

## OTHER INTERESTS

- · Second City -Improv Classes
- · Skiing and Snowboarding
- · Watching lots of movies

## PREDICTIONS

- Channel Launch meeting at 2 p.m.
- Call about a quote and storyboards for Coffee Crisp.
- Post animatics for the next Cartoon Network Spot.
- Confirm a date a time for the Nick Jr. packaging pitch.
- Update schedule for latest Cartoon Network Spot.
- Grit teeth and do horrible petty cash sheet.

## DIARY

Today I know I will be quite busy. I was off Friday; which means a bit of catching up of what happened. We're working on some Halloween packaging for the Cartoon Network and the schedule has been quite insane. In the first 30 sec spot, we have to build (models and set) in 1 week and basically have a week and a half to animate and post. The job is pretty cool and the work makes it worth it. Of course, that's easy for me to say, I'm not the one staying overnight.

I get in and am greeted by a big rush to print out designs for a pitch we are doing at 2 p.m. for an Astral channel launch. Of course, late nights are involved, as well as, a last minute printer crisis and a bit of a kafuffle about where it is safe to spray the toxic glue we need to prepare the presentation boards. I pretty much stay out of it all. Every now and then, I take a quick peek to check in on progress. There isn't too much for me to do other than keep my fingers crossed and act very calm.

ME AND KURT- SELF PORTRAIT!

Surprisingly, I don't have too much email to shuffle through and read. I have to RSVP our group for an YTV (Youth Television) party on Thursday night. We did a bunch of stop-motion interstitials for their promos and in turn, they invited us to their wrap party. The Ottawa Animation Festival is happening too;

therefore, most of our directors are headed there because a few of our pieces are on display. After I check in with one of our Aftereffects artists about possibly coming in the next day to help out, he tells me he isn't sure yet.

After the conversation with him, my frustrations mount and all I can say it, "darn," when I have to cancel the computer tech people coming in because we don't have time they need for us to get off the computers and allow them to work. Now even though something really seems to be wrong with the server, I don't think that it's a wise decision, but sometimes, you have to make an executive decision and stand by it. Canceling is my decision today. Frankly, it is simply the way to handle it. Will this day ever end?

I get a call from the producer at Cartoon Network asking us to track the FedEx we sent out with our master – she hasn't received it yet. I hate these calls, you always except to hear that no one knows where it is or that in some crazy way, it's actually sitting on your desk and no one noticed. This time, it's just late arriving and all is OK.

Next on my list is to call back the producer at Roche McCauley who had sent us some boards for a candy commercial. We sent out a quote the week before for the 3 – 4 second end-tag.

The client wanted to show a chocolate bar cut in half, then coming back together, and finally, the wrapper is to enter from the lower frame and wrap itself around the bar. The team assembles to discuss if we can animate the real bar without it melting under the studio's hot lights. We all realize (early) that this will not be an easy task, just on the debate that still continues. While I talk with my client contact, I realize that I have misunderstood the boards they initially sent. There are two different sets of bars at the end, where I thought they were all for the same commercial. Indeed not! I guess that's what happens when you don't ask enough or the right questions. Anyway – we plan to talk again tomorrow after I have had a chance talk to Drew (the spot's Director) to again discuss what the Client wants and to make sure we have budgeted appropriately. In the original quote, we kept the number low assuming the animation could be quite quick. Now that may have all changed.

Suddenly it's past 1:00 pm (where is the day going?)and Steve (one of the directors in the company) is madly trying to finish his pitch for the new channel launch. I interrupt and ask when we'll be able to post animatics for the next Cartoon Network spot. The part of the job that I hate the most is, (but that I do more than anything else) I stand behind, beside or in front of the directors and animators while they're busy doing something important so I can ask them when, why and how we will do something later in the day. Part of my job is to keep reminding everyone of the schedule and to think ahead, but I realize that I am highly irritating at times, after all, I've been in there positions, looking at a Manager who wants what he wants when he wants it. Never mind what anyone else is doing.

Anyway, we decide to aim for the end of the day and I call the producer (Ashley) to let her know. She asked for about an hour's notice so she can gather all the creative material for us to take a look. I told her that I would try my best, but sometimes when we're this busy, it's hard to know how long something will take.

Drew and I run out to grab some take-out sushi for lunch, and we all manage to eat while the final boards are put together for our channel pitch. I called a cab and Paula (our marketing director/producer) called Astral to tell them that we're running a bit late but are on the way. We arrive and walk into a room with three of the Astral team and the head of their French channels video-conferenced in. This means we're on video on his end.

I take a moment to look at myself on the TV I wonder if I really do have that sallow skin I see. As I glance at everyone *on the screen, I noticed that everyone in the room was looking equally sallow. (So, I sat back realizing that I can ease up on the exercise regime for a minute and concentrate on what was being said).*

*Good News! We have the biggest boards...We rock!*

*The presentation goes great – everyone likes what Steve, Julian and Isaac have done. It's nice to get a warm reaction because sometimes when presenting creative material, people sit and look, completely stone faced even if they've secretly wet their pants with excitement at what you've shown them. The client tells us that we'll be called at the end of the week with some initial decisions. Five companies are pitching for four different channel designs and, ideally, the Astral people hope to assign each company a chunk of the work.*

*We return feeling pretty good. Isaac goes to print out our boards (regular size) so we can courier the pictures to Astral and they can have them for reference. At the same time, Steve asks Isaac to start doing a logo change for another Astral job, which is not due until the end of the month. Why is Isaac panicking and trying to do two things at once? I am caught totally off guard and not sure, where the logo is and exactly what we need to do. That project is planned for next week.*

*Anyway – all easily resolved, logo found, directions clarified, but not before an example how easily one innocent request can throw things off when I think we're doing one thing and someone else another.*

*Suddenly I remember that I should call Sharon at Nickelodeon and see how they want us to present our concepts for the packaging we're presenting on the 11th. I can't get a hold of her and leave a message. She phones back but I'm not in the office, she says we can have a conference call between Oct 11 and 15. I leave her another message asking if we can do 3:00 pm Oct 15th and also ask if we can do a conference call with them ASAP just to clear up their creative needs.*

*Julian is walking out of the door when I remember that I need to pop on the Nick Jr. reference tape that we have and print their 1 page concept sheet. He'll be out all week, but the hope is that he can come up with some ideas while away.*

*Oh yes – the petty cash – well, I was able to throw that in Paula's lap – to Paula's dismay. Of course, she won't allow me to escape without reminding me that I did this last week. Do you think that she's implying that I am making this a habit? We have a great bookkeeper, but she has been on maternity leave. It's amazing how little things like a petty cash sheet can take a*

A ROUGH SKETCH IDEA FOR AN ANIMATED FLY FOR A NEW CHANNEL

chunk out of your day – especially when you don't seem to have as much spent in receipts as money gone. Darn that petty cash!

Where has the day gone? Just a couple of minutes ago, it was 1 and now it's 5. The end of the day has arrived and we have a Cartoon Network meeting scheduled regarding the next deadline with Steve (director), Kyle (postmaster), and Drew (animator). The group realizes that we need to hire someone else for the position of postproduction. I think there is no sense in going through another panic of all nighters or last minute hunts for post-people, when all of this can be handled *beforehand. So, I take the initiative and set-up an interview with a guy named Sasha for tomorrow at noon. Kyle posts our animatic and Steve heads home. I'm almost done for the day when we get a call from Liz, a rep in the Midwest, who tells me about a Lipton Noodle soup job she wants us to go for. They may use a live rooster with replacement mouths or go stop-motion. They're still deciding but hopefully our reel will sway them the stop-motion way. She gives me the three names to send the reels. As Paula and I stuff and address the FedEx packages, Paula (bless her heart) ends up doing more of the work, as I get pulled away to discuss getting an extra drive for storage. Teamwork is what it's all about and Paula and I help each other out like this a lot. It's great to have that back up since there's really just the two of us there doing our designated jobs while answering the phone, sending out reels to clients, and any administrative stuff in between.*

*At 6:30pm, (this is truly a never-ending day), I call the producer at the Cartoon Network to make sure they were able to see the animatics we posted. Great, they viewed it and we schedule a chat at 10 am the next morning.*

*And I do believe that I am done with my day! Oh wait – somewhere in there, I ran out for a piece of pizza. C'est Tout!*

## LESSONS/PROBLEMS

*Whew – that was a bit of a hectic day – not so hectic schedule wise for me – but a ton of little things to check and remember. I'm really happy about what the guys pitched – I think all their ideas were really impressive and original. And at the end, we got a new job opportunity in so – pretty good day (and I didn't have to do the petty cash!). To totally top off my day, I managed to have a slice of pizza for lunch.*

JULIAN, GUARDS THE MANNEQUIN LEGS ON SET WHILE DIRECTING

## PREDICTIONS

- 10 am conference call with Cartoon Network.
- Confirm conference call with Nick Jr. team.
- Get rotoscoped shots from GVFX.
- Interview Aftereffects artist noon.
- New budget sent to Roche McCauley re: candy bar spot.

## DIARY

For some reason when I get in this morning, I still am a bit sleepy. Obviously, not a good night's sleep. As I make some tea and munch on a few chocolate almonds that are lying around, hoping that will perk me up. Thankfully, the conference call scheduled at 10:00 with the Cartoon Network has been delayed until 11 since their copywriter is stuck in an Avid session. We are anxiously waiting on the animatic approval so we can start animating.

Meanwhile, I talk with Kyle our post person, about getting another drive so he can work on his laptop and we could free up a computer to hire another compositor. Really, we need to expand our hub so we can have more people access our drives and server but all that has to wait until after this project is done. It's just too crazy to have any down time due to tech issues. I

*call GVFX, the effects company doing some rotoscoping for us.
One shot is already complete and has been posted on their FTP
site. The remaining shots are to arrive tomorrow. When Kyle
goes in to download it, he realizes that the character is not in
colour – we only have the alpha channels so the character is in
B&W. Once we call GVFX again, they re-render the shot and we
have it an hour later.*

*Finally, I get the Cartoon Network on the phone. It is Steve and
I on one end, and Ashley and the copywriter on the other. The
network is concerned with the duration of the narrative in the
spot. They think it is great to build the story, but part of their
job is to get across the channel's info; therefore, and they need
us to cut 4 – 5 seconds out of the top end of the spot. Cutting is
definitely not going to be an easy task without sacrificing some
good shots or beats. Steve goes to work with Jason (another
compositor) to see what we can do. We promised to have a
re-post of the animatic on our website later today. It's always
hard from the creative standpoint to have to sacrifice in order
to allow for advertising or the informational part of a spot. But,
that's what commercials and promos are all about I guess.*

*Suddenly, it is noon and the Aftereffects artist we are
interviewing has arrived. Wow – time flies sometimes. We have*

*a chat with him in the boardroom and check out his reel. We really like his work! We're trying to decide who to bring on at what is essential – all at the last minute! We are in need of someone who is very familiar with the software and a fast worker. We're still undecided.*

*I pop out to grab some lunch, bring it back and revise the candy spot budget with Steve. We raised the costs to allow for the extra animation, and I faxed it to Leslie, the producer. Then I stop to eat some vegetables that I bought in the frozen food section of Loblaws(a local grocer). They look fresh and delicious on their packaging – let me tell you, they aren't so fresh and delicious and I end up ditching them. I buy some sushi and eat that with some chocolate almonds (every studio should be fully stocked with them because they are a real lifesaver).*

*Isaac finished printing out copies of the Astral boards, and I am just waiting for Steve to check them over before I send them over. We have to be sure the color and layout look good.*

*Meanwhile, I call and leave a message for Sharon at Nick Jr. (again) to set-up the conference call. She's still out of the office. I go back through my notes and find the number of the artistic director and call him. Lucky for me he answers and we schedule the call for tomorrow at 11 am. This ends up changing about*

*3 times over the next hour as all of us try to co-ordinate our schedules. FINALLY, we decide on noon. The new schedule works out well because Steve has to leave at 2pm for the Ottawa Animation Festival.*

*We still haven't decided whether to hire the compositor person we interviewed this morning on this particular job. We think his skills may be more animation suited than compositing. Steve and I decide to call someone else we've dealt with but he's unavailable. He gives me the name of a friend of his and I set up a meeting for 9:30 tomorrow. Cutting it a little bit close – poor Steve – his morning will be jam packed between meetings and overseeing The Cartoon Network project.*

*We post a new animatic for the Cartoon Network folk around 4 pm – they're fine with it. Now we just have to post the cut-down :23 sec and :15 sec animatics. I remember that we need to FedEx them a Dbeta tape with the missing greenscreen shot from Friday's delivery. So, I choose that as my task. I also call Dave at GVFX about the promised quote for making a prop coffee crisp – he claims he'll get it to me ASAP.*

*The day ends with a few last minute phone calls and a run to FedEx. Quickly, I grab half a sub from Subway on my way to FedEx, nothing like easting on the run. I have to move because my gym class starts at 7 p.m. But, I can't go home without doing just a little grocery shopping.*

## LESSONS/PROBLEMS

*With all that is going on at the studio lately, I am a bit nervous with everyone leaving for the animation festival. But, it's always a nice reward to be able to go see your work acknowledged so I'm glad their going – just bad timing.*

THE DOOR TO THE OFFICE!

Day 3 | **OCTOBER 2**

## PREDICTIONS

· *Crazy day as Steve has to leave at 2 pm.*

· *Nick Jr. conference call at noon.*

· *Interview at 9:30/hire compositor.*

· *Organize everything so that we can still function with half the crew going to the Ottawa festival for the rest of the week.*

· *Get our roto stuff back ASAP.*

## DIARY

*I get in late and we have a 9:30 interview. Well, not late
– about 9:20 but I thought there'd be people waiting outside a
locked door. Power went out in half the apartment and I was
trying to dry my hair in the reflection of the kitchen cupboard.
Anyway, apparently the morning commute is bad because
Steve and Max (interviewee) are late as well. So – we talked
to Max. All went well and I think we'll hire him on for the next
week and a half. The major problem is we now have lots of post
people – but we are losing our animator! Drew is leaving for
the Ottawa animation festival tomorrow and is trying to pump
out as much work as possible before he takes off, so these guys
have a lot of stuff to work on (to put it mildly).*

*We're still trying to figure out what computer Max will use when
he starts. We have decided that Kyle will use his laptop, but still
the problem is that we have no more room on the hub to let
Kyle access the server (which is still dysfunctional). Anyway – I
am finally going to try and get some tech guys in to maybe add
another hub and fix the server.*

*We received contracts from Nickelodeon to sign in regards to
the pitch for Nick Jr. Steve and I looked them over and Steve
signed them. I made up a FedEx pack to send them back.*

*He'll be taking off any minute. I also received a call from a production company in Vancouver who were interested in Steve as a live-action director after seeing the IKEA "Heads" spot. I explained that sadly Steve comes with the whole Head Gear package. It sounds as though the spot may be animated and so she asked that I send her a reel. It's so great that the IKEA spot is getting loads of attention.*

*After lunch, I return several emails – quick stuff about credits for a spot we did and a check-in with Astral to make sure they got the boards I sent last night. I also call Cartoon Network to let them know we have posted the cut-down versions of our animatic. We haven't heard back yet. Suddenly it is 2:30. Yikes. I still have to go to the bank and pay my darn taxes. While I am thinking about it, I am going to run out right now.*

*Well, not only did I get some errands done – I got some treats for everyone. October is such a great month for Halloween mini-candies. Drew is making weird noises like a duck right now and it keeps reminding me of a cat throwing up. Other than that, things have really calmed down this afternoon. The tech guy is coming in tomorrow to check out the hub and the server – yeah! Drew is on hold from animating because he is waiting for a prop Meagan is making. He's only going to be able to set*

---

*up the shot today because we have to post the lighting and framing the website for Steve's approval. Steve says he'll check in the morning.*

*I sit with Isaac for a bit and go over some of his designs for the Nick Jr. pitch. They are requesting that we design a "Nick Jr. Land" that will encompass entirely new packaging for their big TV block. They want to unite all the different shows by putting their character in one similar environment between programs. Isaac's ideas look great – we talk about some ways to lead into each show open using his style and concepts.*

*Oh no! I forgot to call the Cartoon Network to ask about our first payment. It's good to check in on these things once in awhile (squeaky wheel and so on), and it also helps me know how to budget for the next while. It's past 5pm so I'll do that tomorrow. I'm just going to write my to-do list for tomorrow and then go home. 5:45, pretty good. I usually like to do my to-do list the night before as I'm less likely to forget any little things I need to follow up on for the next day. And it gives a good sense of closure.*

## LESSONS/PROBLEMS

*Today was one of those days that started out at a crazy pace and then kind of slowed in the afternoon. This is really nice, except you always get a weird feeling, you forgot to do something. I think Steve and I feel pretty good about delivering our next spot in a week – we have hired extra post people and Drew has managed to shoot a fair amount of animation for them to work on before he leaves for the festival.*

*Let's see how calm I am next Wednesday night!*

## PREDICTIONS

· Call regarding our first payment from Cartoon Network.

· Make sure we get all our roto footage.

· Get tech guy in to install new hub.

## DIARY

*Well, today seems to be a laid-back day. The week is getting a bit more relaxed as it goes on – which is always nice! I get in and do the usual checking of my email. Apparently, our roto footage should be here about noon.*

*Steve calls in about 11 am to check out what Drew has set up for the next Cartoon Network shot. He approves it but there is a bit of a debate as to how fast the zombies should be moving and where they should be looking. Drew and Steve thought we could maybe wait until Monday to do the shot, but both Kyle and I agree it is important to try and get it done today – there is still too much stuff to be done next week – and we'll only have four days. There always seems to be a crunch no matter how well you plan.*

*We get the CD from GVFX with our rotoscoped footage but it doesn't contain the alpha channel Kyle needs. Now we have to* wait until tomorrow to get the CD back with everything fixed. That's bit of a drag. The guys can use the footage we have and replace it later, but it still makes for extra work in the end.

I talk to Ashley at the Cartoon Network about our check and apparently, it had just gone through today. If she can get it signed and FedEx'd out tomorrow, we'll have it Monday. Perfect. It's always exciting to receive money!

About 1:00pm, I take my lunch break. I have been meaning to replace my alarm clock for about 2 weeks and guess what – today is the day! Now this is exciting! I do think there will be more variety in the drugstore.

It's amazing how many different types of alarm clocks you can find in the drugstore at such a nominal price. I upgrade my alarm clock with a snooze button for less than what I paid for my present clock. To top it off, I find more exciting Halloween mini-chocolate bars – but I just bought a big stash of those yesterday – must have willpower...

By the time I get back, Paula, Drew and Isaac are nearly ready to leave for The Ottawa Animation Festival. I also get a call from Michael the accountant for whom I am supposed to have emailed some check info for year-end balancing. Darn – I totally forgot. I make sure that I do that task right away, only to discover that Paula emailed him everything he needs only moments before. Oh well – at least he has what he needs.

The tech guy shows up and installs the new hub. The reason our server is slow, he thinks, it's because not all of our computers are upgraded to the 10.1 MAC platform. I don't even know if Paula's computers and mine can handle the 10.1 platform. My computer can't handle opening QuickTime files. It's almost 5pm and I seem to be done doing what I need. Maybe I can take off a bit early. I have a few things to do after work and then I'm meeting some people to go to a Comedy Show hosted by one of the guys that worked here for a bit on YTV. And then – we're all going to the YTV party together. It should be fun.

## LESSONS/PROBLEMS

It was a pretty quiet day. With everyone gone, even though all the deadlines are the same, you have to kind of slow down. This gave me a chance to catch up on paperwork, and filing and the rest of the "stuff" that falls by the wayside otherwise.

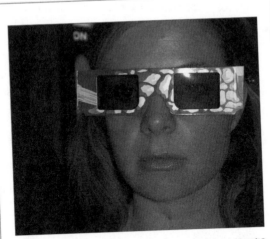

ME, IN THE GLASSES I WEAR TO GREET CLIENTS

Day 5 | **OCTOBER 4**

## PREDICTIONS

- Pretty slow day, everyone is away.
- Get roto stuff that is being re-done.

## DIARY

The week has come to a slow halt. With Steve gone, we can only work on the stuff we have, so there is not a lot for me to do today. We all get in a bit late after being at the YTV party last night; which was a blast of an event. I didn't arrive at the party until after 10:30 to find that it was in full swing. Food and open bar. Delightful.

I have a lunch meeting today with the producer that has optioned the children's series I wrote with my writing partner Mary. This is a good day for it, since I didn't feel too stressed about being away from the office. We were brought up to date on what is happening with the show and it seems that it's been getting a good reception – which is exciting. We're in the process of getting a development deal. Mary and I are trying not to get too excited in case it all falls through. It's so hard not to imagine yourself on a yacht with a servant – and a vat of Swiss chocolate (just for a sec).

When I get back from lunch, everyone is busy working and it seems oddly quiet. I check our general Head Gear information email and look at some people's resumes, and email them back. I usually try to email people that drop off tapes and portfolios if I can. Unfortunately, it gets a bit too busy sometimes. I also am surprised that many people who apply here do not seem to know about the work we do. We get tons of people applying for 3D/CGI positions and really, we don't do that here. So, there's my little lesson of the day: investigate the company you're *sending your application! Why waste a demo reel if you don't have to?*

*Ashley calls and asks us to send the raw elements from the Cartoon shoot when we send our next batch of material. I ask Kyle about doing that – it's only a problem in that it means we have to render out those 11 or 12 shots again – and that takes time! At this point, we don't have half of that to give. Maybe we can send the stuff a little later or something. I'll have to give her a shout and see how badly they need it.*

*The most exciting call of the day is from Heather at Astral Media. She calls around 4 pm to say that they really like the pitch ideas we have for the new channels (that presentation was on Monday). She confirms that we're definitely into the next stage. She says they're presenting stuff to the "higher ups" next Wednesday and will call Thursday to let us know what they want to move forward and develop. So – I'm pretty excited, to say the very least. What a great way to end the week!*

## LESSONS/PROBLEMS

*Hmmm, what can I say? Sometimes it's nice to sit back and have a slow day. Especially when I know, next week will be a bit mad. I'm glad we've got as many post people on board as possible so we'll just have to push through everything. And hopefully next week we get chosen to do some cool stuff for Astral. A big job, but it would be great to have something to go into right after we finish the Cartoon Network.*

## PREDICTIONS

- Confirm schedule for Cartoon – post/shoot.
- Look at invoices for Cartoon Network – pay.
- Call Leslie at Roche re: candy spot.

## DIARY

Ok. I get in around 9:30. Everyone is back and that is so nice. Apparently the Ottawa Animation Festival was quite fun and we won in our category (Children's educational) for our Sesame Street spot "Mr.Roboto" directed by our own Steve Angel! Quite exciting!

Steve has to check Drew's animation that he hasn't seen and catches up on the post work that's happening. I catch up with Paula about any calls and marketing stuff that has happened while she was away. There's really nothing major, as we both have to stop and reminisce about the relaxed days at the end of last week. We go over some of the reels we have sent out and decide who will follow up on what.

I have a bunch of invoices from the post house where we are working on The Cartoon Network to go through, so I double check everything and send over a P.O. to approve billing. I also print and put aside a few invoices I have received from freelancers for our check run on Thursday. Julian reminds me that he and Steve weren't been paid on their last paydays, so I do that and then also remember to do the monthly parking checks for Steve and Julian.

I am so displaced today (as we all are) because we have a small office with only a few desks. I am in the only room (aside from the boardroom) that has a door. So when people have to have private conversations I get booted out of my desk.

Steve's computer is being used by Nick to post the Cartoon Network stuff so he is floating around a bit today as well. We actually have another space upstairs that we'll be renting in November so hopefully that will allow us to spread out a bit. The idea is that one space will be the shooting/building/ production space and the other will be post-production/design and office. It's hard not to have any privacy all day – especially when things are stressful. It can also be fun to be so open-concept but there is no escape at times. Except for greedy me with the office!

Just before lunch, I go over the delivery schedule with Steve, Drew and Kyle. We originally thought we'd need only two people for the final element delivery (Oct. 24) but there are *quite a few things to complete and I'm a bit worried about being short-handed. I suggest we have someone available just in case. Drew is going to be animating madly for the next week and a half. Then, he should get a break. The Cartoon promos are already airing I've heard. I don't have cable at home, so I haven't seen them, but from what I hear, they look good.*

*Aaaah lunch. I am proud of my healthy lunch that consists of a healthy wrap and pineapple dessert that I had time to make last night. I also plan to run out to look for a gift for my nephew, but no luck. No Pooh Bears to be found on Queen Street.*

*The first week in November, I have to take a week off and have been feeling awkward about it since every time I take time off on a week that appears to be free and clear, some huge development or deadline arises. I am keeping my fingers crossed because I simply can't change it. This time, though, I officially wrote it on the calendar, so no one can say he/she didn't know. My brother and his girlfriend have been begging me to come and visit them in Omaha. Maybe I can squeeze in a few more days off at the end of the month, but I can make no promises. Don't you just hat how work cuts into vacation time?*

*Late in the afternoon, there's a bit of a panic because we realize we have forgotten to include one shot in the roto's we need* from GVFX. They're way too swamped to do them for us now. Darn. I hope that Nick will be done compositing the last four bumpers tonight and be able to do it tomorrow. Yet another example of how important it is to double-check everything.

The day winds down with a visit from our bookkeeper, Robin, bringing in her new baby who is so cute – and suddenly so hungry! Steve gets in a little practice playing around with her. After all, he'll have his own new baby in a few weeks (or is it a month?). After Robin leaves, I remember to call Leslie about the candy job – to see if she understands the quote or has any questions but I just get her voicemail. Hopefully she'll call tomorrow. A compositor drop by who is looking for an intern position. His main software is Aftereffects so that's great. He seems like a good guy, Steve and I chat with him for a bit. It's always good to meet people – sometimes it's really hard to judge someone from a resume, so I never mind taking a few minutes to chat if people can come down.

Paula is away the next couple days so we just catch up on any calls she is expecting, back up our database and that is that. I eat dinner and now I am off to my class. I take Improv on Monday nights. C'est tout.

NICK SITTING AT A WORK STATION, COMPOSITING

## LESSONS/PROBLEMS

The only thing I can think of is, although the day went pretty smoothly, it was a big pain in the butt not to have had that one particular roto shot done. And as I said, even if you think everyone else has double-checked something, it's always worth a third look. If this had been discovered tomorrow afternoon, we would have really been in a tight spot.

## PREDICTIONS

· We'll see how well we're doing with finishing Cartoon Network – only 2 days to go.
· Call Heather at Astral re: logo change for MoviePix.
· Make an element delivery/tape schedule for our Thursday output.

## DIARY

I am so tired today. I think I may be catching a cold and am having a hard time getting motivated. Paula is off today and tomorrow (as I mentioned) and it's quite quiet as Julian and Isaac are working in the boardroom on a pitch for Nick Jr., and everyone else is working on the Cartoon Network project. Drew is in the shooting space trying to get three shots done today so I doubt we'll see much of him at all.

As I always do, I check my email first thing, Nothing really to report. I also check the Head Gear General information box. There's always tons of stuff in there – most of it junk mail, but people do send reel requests or resumes so Paula and I try and alternate checking it. It's so second nature to check your own email, but when it gets busy, you have to really make a note to check that stuff.

No word from the message I left in regards to the candy spot. I try to phone again but no answer, so I just leave a brief message. Some time ago we sent the Midwest representative, Liz, a bunch of reels (per her request) and I haven't heard a word from her since. To be on the safe side, I send her a "touch base" email.

I talk to Steve about how the shots are going and what state they're in. He suggests that when I chat with Kyle about our status, we make a sheet up of all the things that need to be completed for each shot. So we have an easy reference. I do as Kyle requests and we sit down and go through everything. According to him, all the shots are only about 75% there and yet, he is not freaking out, amazing!

HEY! Where's the Cartoon Network check we are supposed to get this week? I'd better look into that. It might still be stuck in the machine over there waiting for a signature. I saw an article in Animation Magazine online with a press release for this big Halloween carton marathon that they are doing (for which we are doing the promos. Unfortunately, neither the promos nor Head Gear are mentioned. Bah Humbug. (Is it too early for that?)

About 12:15 I go out to the Blood Donor clinic, I automatically re-book when I'm there and I almost forgot about this appointment. Anyway – I get there, wait in line and then the nurse tells me my iron is too low. Can you believe they are rejecting me? I beg them to take my blood. "What's the worst that could happen," I ask. The nurse refuses to even answer that one. Oh well. I walk around the mall a bit to cheer up my blood, and return to the office.

I return to discover that Liz has emailed to say that the chicken soup people have decided to go CG and so they are bidding through other companies. Bah Humbug again! I can't help myself, "darn the competition!"

The production company in Vancouver has also decided to do their animation elsewhere. Their decision is based more on location than anything else and they really enjoyed our reel.

We also find out today that Kyle, our post-whiz is taking a permanent job at another company. Sad news for us, Kyle really knows this place inside out and he's part of the Head Gear family. It will be a good move for him, so we're happy for him. It also will only be on the floor below us so he'll still be around for visitations. We're going to have to get all his Head Gear t-shirts back though...

Around 5 pm, I give our Playback contact a call to follow up for Paula. She has been interested in doing an interview with some of the director's that have worked in The Ottawa Animation Festival. She said that she has talked to the festival director and has gotten all the information that she needs. I'm just going to email her some stills in the morning.

The only big thing left to do is have another quick meeting with Kyle and Steve to see where we're at with the shots. Hopefully, that will make me feel pretty good. Steve is just setting up a shot with Drew and then we should be able to do this...

Well, it all seems to be under control – but even just rendering each shot with its different green screen passes will take a long time. I'm hoping to be able to have a third of the shots on tape by end of day tomorrow. Fingers crossed!

### LESSONS/PROBLEMS

It's always exciting to have your reel sent out for a job but you send so many, and get a lot of bites that never turn into anything. It's a bit disappointing – but also good to know that people know about us at least. Maybe next time.

## PREDICTIONS

· Everyone will suddenly feel very stressed as we realize how much work there is to do.
· Figure out the tape log, make tape labels, and prep for Friday delivery.
· Call Heather about Movie Pix.
· Sesame Street Stills to Playback.
· Invoice Nick JR.
· Order tape stock maybe.
· What the heck is wrong with the printer?

## DIARY

The weather is getting brisk and fall like. It makes me want to stay in bed – which I should have done longer since the subway broke down and I was late getting in this morning anyway. I bump into Drew on the way in – he's as sick as a dog, but he dragged himself in to finish shooting the Cartoon Network. It's been a crazy month and a half, everyone has been working overtime and weekends and it hasn't been easy. Once we deliver Friday, we'll be in the home stretch.

Kyle and I sit down and go through all the shots again so I can make up a master list of what order and at what Time code they all need to be put on tape. This way, even if we render them out as finals out of order, I still know where to put them on the Dbeta. This will definitely help with organization. I also make a lovely chart for us to check the stages of approval as we progress. We have 28 shots to complete and render by tomorrow night. It seems that all the big stuff is done and hopefully now it's just tweaking.

I make up the tape and labels for our initial element run just to get that out of the way. I'll finish up all the final paperwork and FedEx tomorrow. I've got to now remember to invoice Nick Jr. I call Sharon the producer and she passes me off to their accounting department. So, I touch base with them and fax the invoice. Now, I can cross that off my list.

We don't have much stock left and that could really be a problem. In fact, we only have a few six minute DBETAS and barely any VHS. I'm going to need more for Friday so I order it right away – that's the kind of stuff you forget to do and then go to reach for a tape – and there's none there! The supplier promises to get everything to us tomorrow via FedEx.

Lunchtime and it's roti! Yum…roti is always so filling. It's the perfect comfort food to make you feel sleepy two hours after you eat. I make myself some tea and clean up the kitchen area a bit. It is then that I decide to deal with our broken printer. No *one really knows what's wrong with it – it just doesn't work and has been sitting like that for months. I am thinking we should send it to the repair place at Epson and see if they can fix it before we spend a bunch of money on a brand new model. It'll probably take a couple weeks to hear back so best to deal with it immediately.*

*Around 3 pm I ask Kyle if we can go over the list of what is complete and ready for Steve's approval and what can go out to tape. He is just finishing off a few things so we probably get to it around 3:30. Most of the stuff is ready for Steve's approval although it will probably all require tweaking. The bumpers are all done and ready to go onto tape though and hopefully Steve will give a stamp of approval. He's just on the phone so we'll have to wait for him to finish up.*

*I've had a couple people drop by today. An illustrator dropped by with a resume and some samples of his work. I talk to him for a bit and say I'll try to set up something with Julian once this madness is over in a few weeks. Paul, a compositor we'd like to work, with also comes by. We've had opposing schedules so far – in that he's busy whenever we need him, or we're not when he's free. He may be free in December so hopefully we'll get one of the Astral jobs we're bidding and we can bring him on.*

*Okay, it's 5 pm and the bumpers are ready and approved for Dbeta. I suggest that we throw them onto VHS and send them to The Cartoon Network guys since they haven't seen anything thus far. This takes a half hour of confusion and trying to work around the Dbeta downstairs so the tape isn't assembled as neatly as I would like. At least they're going out.*

*Turns out the computer Max is working on is working in slow motion and Max is stuck doing our most complex scene at the moment. We contemplate moving all the files to Jason's computer but after talking to him, Max thinks he'll be done in half an hour. I am feeling the stress. There is a lot to do and I'm afraid it'll be a late night for everyone. I can't do a lot to help, except try and keep everything organized. I also can pace...right behind everyone as they work. I find that's always appreciated.*

*Well, we work out some sort of a plan – Steve's coming back around 9pm to hopefully approve stuff and I'll call in to see how everything is going. Down to the last 24 hours.*

*I call in at about 11 pm. Steve has come in to approve everything. Apparently, Kyle and Steve are able to assemble all the shots and edit them into the master 30-second sequence. This will save us a lot of time laying the shots to tape tomorrow and will make the edit on Friday MUCH easier. The only catch is the render. Kyle isn't going to stay at work until 4 am to make sure the render doesn't crash, but that long a render can often just stop. Aaah well, we'll have to see.*

## LESSONS/PROBLEMS

*We're looking good but there really is no room for error on this job. Everything is so perfectly timed. I'm REALLY happy the shots got edited into the full 30-second sequence – that is amazing. I am nervous about the render screwing up overnight.*

## PREDICTIONS

· Prepare tapes and labels for Cartoon delivery.
· Make Dbeta master of Cartoon Network.
· Do payroll.
· Check in with Astral.

## DIARY

I am nervous as I enter the building wondering whether the overnight render worked or just kacked out on us. When I walk in, Kyle and Steve are at the computer and I must have a look of trepidation on my face because they ask what's wrong (I hope I didn't look that way the whole subway ride).

Exciting news, everything worked and we are all ready to go to tape(we render our shots to a digital storage device called the Accom and from there we lay off to the Dbeta which is owned by the company below us – Topix).

There are a few scenes that need to be fixed, but we could just insert those into the sequence and not have to redo everything. So that's what is going to happen – I will go sit in my office and relax. We are actually in pretty good shape. I check my email and messages and follow up on those. Then I do all the tape labels and get all the blank tapes ready that we will need tomorrow. I also update the Time code log that I had done the previous day. Now that we have been able to assemble the 30 sequence, the time codes from yesterday are irrelevant.

Kyle and I go over our progress chart so I know exactly what is done and what we are still waiting on. In the meantime, I tell Paula I can do paychecks this week, since my day isn't that busy, until we are ready to output. We do our payroll every two weeks and Paula and I usually do it – whoever has the time. I have a few invoices to pay from some freelance work the week before and then the regular check run.

Steve comes into my office to see if Heather from Astral has called. We are all anticipating hearing how their presentation went the day before. Apparently, they are deciding on whom they will award the broadcast design. Just as we begin discussing whether I should phone her, the phone rings and it's Heather. With what she says is, "good news, and news that she hopes the guys (Steve and Julian) will think is good". That's all she will give away other than we've definitely been awarded one of the jobs. She asks if she and Fillip (the art director) can come by Friday at 11:30. I don't have our schedules memorized and I am afraid Steve and I will still be at the color correct, but there isn't another time they can make it. Therefore, it is set up.

After lunch, Paula and I go over all the invoices of the last month and catch up on some accounting. I also realize FedEx had arrived and we still don't have the Cartoon Network check, so I email Ashley. She put a trace on it and only to find it has been routed to Montreal! Well, at least it has crossed the border. She assures me we'll have it on Friday. We also get a call from a local production company asking for a reel; apparently, they are looking for someone to do a show opening. Fairly soon it sounds like, Paula offers to send it out for me.

By the late afternoon things are getting busy. I don't think I'll have time to get any drinks or snacks for the Astral meeting. I have to make sure we have all the elements that we need for tomorrow. Paula offers to go out to get some food AND clean up the boardroom so we are now ready for the next day.

I am trying to co-ordinate with Topix as to when we can use their Dbeta . We have realized that for one of the packaging elements we need a clean plate that hasn't been rendered. Kyle finishes all of that and we are ready. I went down to the tape room, and found that there was another client in there also doing some final Dbeta work. I am slightly annoyed because I *am made to wait for her (as she explains to me, "she is trying to make a deadline"). I wait (impatiently), but finally get everything onto tape at 7pm. That's the only problem about not having a Dbeta machine (which is crazily expensive and doesn't make sense or us to have since we are hooked up to the one downstairs) when time is crucial, waiting for it drives me insane. Oh well. It is finished and on tape and in my bag ready for color correct. Steve and I agree to meet at Mag North – the post house – at 9am in the morning. The most stressful part is over and oh yah! The spot looks great. Hope they like it!*

### LESSONS/PROBLEMS

*Even hours after wanting to tell someone like the "I have deadline so I need the Dbeta" woman to go away, I still am happy with the decision to smile politely and step aside. I can only hope that my voodoo curse will cause her FedEx to be delayed a day. Oh yes, it feels great to leave work knowing that we won't have an overnight mad work thing because all the finished tapes are in my bag! Yeah!*

JULIAN AND DREW GOOF AROUND WITH THE
COSTUMES WHILE ON SET

THE CHANNEK 2 SOCK PUPPET WITH OUR HEAD
GEAR LOGO

## PREDICTIONS

- Astral meeting 11:30.
- Color Correct, On Line 9 am and 2 pm.
- FedEx Nick Jr. and Cartoon Network.

## DIARY

*I go directly to the post house in the morning where I'm
meeting Steve for the color correct session at 9:00 am. I get
there and the colorist is just finishing some dailies and is
running a bit behind, he asks if we can wait 20 minutes. It
probably wouldn't have been a big deal except for the 11:30
Astral meeting we have, so I ask them to finish after we are
done, which they are great about. I actually worked at Mag
North about five years ago so I always have lots of catching
up to do with the people I used to work with. Steve arrives just
after 9am and points out that we didn't bring our previous
master to match the color (darn! Moreover, I even double-
checked that I had picked up everything last night). Steve
makes a mad dash to his bike and rides back to work – faster
than if I was to take a cab amidst tons of construction.*

*We get started about 20 minutes later and this session goes
a lot quicker than the first since we have the spot already*

*assembled (makes it much easier to make sure all the color match shot to shot). We also have four bumpers to color correct and then three extended shots, which we will use to edit the various versions. Surprisingly we are done before 11 am and make it back to work well before the Astral meeting. I leave all our tapes at Mag North since we are going back there for edit at 2pm.*

*Back at Head Gear, Isaac and Julian are working away on our pitch for Nick Jr. The stills and boards are looking great. I hope they would finish by the end of the day and not have to work on the weekend – this is a long weekend in Canada, Thanksgiving, so we have Monday off. Heather calls to say that they will be held up a little bit and they arrive about 11:30. So – the good news – we basically have been asked to do 2 out of 5 channels, which is really exciting. We haven't agreed to it yet, for a few reasons, one being that the deadline for delivery for all the channels is early January – a deadline that would be tight if only doing one, so obviously don't want to commit without figuring out how to complete all the work. Both the channels need to be redesigned – they want to change direction from what we originally presented.*

The first channel is based on Julian's designs. The second channel we are doing will be completely re-designed based on some internal ideas at Astral. We have a good meeting, and it is exciting to be awarded two jobs, now we just have to discuss the practical. But, it'll have to wait since Steve and I need to grab some food and head back to Mag North.

So, we are back around 2 pm in the AVID suite assembling everything. Steve stays long enough to see everything timed properly and then heads back to work. We still have a fourth delivery for The Cartoon Network and he needs to do some cel animation so Kyle and Jason can keep progressing with post. I stay while we on-line the edited sequences downstairs, put in the slates, and make the dubs I need. I end up taking the streetcar back to work because as I mentioned, traffic sucks. I get back about 4 pm.

First thing, I prepare the paperwork, a note to Ashley at the Cartoon Network and put together that FedEx. I also complete the FedEx that we are sending to Nickelodeon, it contains a VHS of the Sesame Street spot "Up N Down" which they have seen a clip of on our reel and really like. As soon as I am finished, I go to drop off the FedEx(s). I still have an hour before pick up, but I just feel better having them dropped off and out of the

way. What a great feeling it is to have everything out of the
door. I email Ashley at the Cartoon Network to give her the
tracking number if she needed it Monday and remind her we
are away today day as well. I leave my home number just in
case there is an emergency and the tape got lost. I do have
a clone of the Master I can resend. I send a similar email to
Sharon at Nick Jr. with almost an identical message.

We then have a brief conversation as to how we will be able
to do 2 channels by early January, we throw around the idea
that it may be better to concentrate on one and do it well.
It also depends on the budget since we'd have to get extra
workstations and freelancers. I'd have to do a schedule as well.
Heather is going to get us the deliverables on Tuesday so we'd
have to have the final discussion then. We also have to consider
that we might be moving into a new space in November, which
will make timing difficult. Anyway, we'd figure it out once we
have more information.

It is the weekend and everyone is heading out. It has been a
good day – delivering Cartoon Network, getting a new job and
the Nick Jr. stuff looks good. Isaac and Julian would probably
be in on Monday to do some work and post everything on the
website though. I left at 6pm to go meet a friend for a drink

and then home to pack to go up North for the long weekend.
Ooh, I can't wait for turkey!

## LESSONS/PROBLEMS

After a lot of hard work this was a fairly stress free day for
everyone, and a day where we were awarded more work, a
pretty good feeling heading into the weekend!

# OCTOBER 14

*THANKSGIVING IN CANADA*

A FEW CHARACTERS WE DESIGNED AND BUILT FOR THE LATEST YTV BUMPERS.

Day 11 | *OCTOBER 15*

## PREDICTIONS

- Did the tape get to Cartoon Network?
- Drew shoots the rest of the bumpers.
- Astral meeting and schedule.
- Nick Jr. Pitch at 2:00 pm.

## DIARY

Everyone seems to have had a nice weekend surrounded by eating so much that we are all still recovering from having to get up for work. I don't think 3 pieces of dessert in one sitting was abnormal – well, it seemed reasonable on the weekend.

I am the last one in and Julian and Isaac have posted almost all the Nick Jr. material. I check it on my computer – it's one of the slowest in the office so I like to make sure I can see everything – which is a good test to see if the client will be able to check it out if they have an older system they're using. All looks good. The only thing I can't see is the storyboards – not sure why. Julian is re-working the treatment, so I wait to call Sharon and Manny at Nick Jr. We had posted the storyboards, the treatment, 3 stills of various points in Nick Jr., playland and then a few drawings that explain how the camera will move through the land and how the different layers of the animation would be divided and show depth. When it is all done I leave Sharon a message and get a hold of Manny to let him know the web address of where to look.

In the meantime, we try to discuss the Astral projects. It's been difficult to get us all together with Steve doing cel drawing for the Cartoon Network and Julian and Isaac doing the Nick Jr.

stuff. We're having the most trouble with the idea for Channel 1 – not just trying to make it unique but using the style Heather and Fillip showed us they like. The problem is there is the possibility it could involve a fairly in-depth shoot, which will be a lot of time and money, neither of which are really available for this project. I've leave Heather another message just to get the final deliverables and a ballpark budget. It's always easier to figure out creatively what's possible if we get a ballpark number to work with because it always affects the approach.

I check in with Kyle to see how the last Cartoon stuff is coming along. I am not sure if we will need Nick (another compositor) to come in. Kyle thinks we're doing pretty well and that he and Jason should be able to cover it without a problem. I'll check in again with him tomorrow. I also email Ashley to see if they got the new Cartoon Master since I haven't heard from her. I'm assuming no news is good news, but I'd love to be sure. I know that they have a small window of time to comp in clips, do sound design and prep everything for air once they get our tape so I'm sure she's running around as if she's mad, just happy to have it in her hands.

After lunch I go to the bank to deposit our Cartoon Network payment hoping there won't be a big line since we have the

Nick Jr. meeting at 2:00, only a half hour away. I get back just in time, they phone just after 2pm and Steve, Julian, Isaac and I sit in on the call. Isaac leads the pitch, he is a bit nervous because he hasn't had a lot of experience doing that but he did a great job. Sharon and Manny seems to like what we present.

The two of them had been able to look at the work earlier, which really helped as we talked about it. It was beneficial to go through the boards/layouts with them because there were a few points that I think they may have misunderstood and we were able to clarify.

Sharon and Manny are presenting the pitches on Thursday and then again on Tuesday. She asks for an animated example of what we are showing – just to be able to demonstrate the style, depth and parallax Isaac and Julian to have in the style more clearly. But wait, the tape I sent to them on Friday does everything that they are asking. Since Sharon is asking for the tape, she must not have received it. I promise to track it after the call – which I do, and I believe it is sitting in their mailroom. So, all is good. Now all we have to do is wait to see the outcome.

Meanwhile I have some social co-coordinating to do. Do I mention the dinner we are going to have as an "YTV/Cartoon

Network-Kyle-send-off"? Anyway, between the six people in the office someone always has a conflict with some specific day. This has been dragging on forever. We finally agree on October 29, Tuesday night. I email everyone and call any freelance people that want to attend. I'll worry about where to go later.

As I write this, I remember a crazy busy day, but it doesn't seem that crazy in the writing. There are so many little things that happen sometimes that take a few minutes that you forget what they all are. I know at the end of the day, Steve and Julian discuss the Astral ideas more – we decide I would try and check out some stock footage stills to see if we could actually find good shots to use.

Paula and I try to figure out what we can send new-Mom Robin to her home for bookkeeping work. We finally decide she will have to come in and sort it out herself. We email her to see what she thought about that proposal. Paula is off Friday and Monday so her desk is free. We have the monthly statements and stuff, which is due for August/September and the accountant is asking for them. Paula and I can do them, but Robin sounds like she doesn't mind a few hours of work – so don't let us stand in the way!!! Anyway, I am leaving today at *about 6:30 or something, thinking that there seems to be a million things left to do.*

## LESSONS/PROBLEMS

*Today was one of those days where for a while I seem to be waiting to do something, and then suddenly a few hours pass and I can't even remember what details had me so occupied. The day was a bit fragmented working between the Nick Jr. pitch, Cartoon Network, and the Astral discussions and I still kind of feel like nothing was resolved. I mean the pitch went well, but now we're waiting for a response. I guess I'm not very patient!*

PRELIMINARY SKETCH FOR A 70'S BASEMENT SET DREW IS CREATING.

## PREDICTIONS

· *Must resolve Astral budget, schedule.*
· *Must complete Movie pix logo change.*
· *Get some stock footage samples.*
· *Order cake for Paula's birthday.*

## DIARY

*Aaaah – Wednesday. How on earth do you spell Wednesday? There's crazy tricky "e" in there. I have a block against this day – it's like the word "squirrel" in the first grade spelling bee. Lots of stress over that I recall. I actually spelled it right in the end and then lost because I spelled "of" as "o-v". Poor little me the loser. ANYWAY – little aside…*

*Poor Paula is feeling sick, in fact sicker than yesterday, she's got some sort of flu and is supposed to be recuperating for her weekend away, not getting worse. It also ranges from freezing cold in the office, to wickedly hot when the heat is on. That can't be helping. Anyway, my first duty of the day is to call Dufflet Pastry and order a delicious Lemon Parfait cake for tomorrow – Paula's birthday is on the weekend. We all love the lemon parfait cake; it's almost like a child to us really, I mean, any cake is quite beloved around here but this one holds a special place. Just to make sure we have plenty, Paula and I decide that to be safe we really need the large.*

*That big task out of the way, I give Heather a call but end up leaving a message again. I think she been in meetings all day, so the phone tag starts. Since we still don't have a full list of deliverables, we can't do a proper budget but I might as well do a schedule. It seems obvious that if we did two channels we'd have to have two separate teams of people working on them concurrently. I decide to do a rough schedule on my own and then sit down with Steve and Julian to revise it. Well, about two seconds after I look at it I realize I need them to help me, since I'm not sure how much design time vs. shoot/animation etc... we will need. Steve's busy finishing the cel animation for Kyle, so Julian and I got through it and figure out what seems to be a tight but doable schedule. We'd ask for an extra week to deliver the initial elements (mid Jan.) and then the rest of the packaging at the end of the month.*

*I've also put a call into a couple stock footage places. One of them gives me a website pass and says they'll put together some stills for us that we can view in a couple hours. We need people involved in leisure activities, ideally, we'd get a series of photos of the same event. Sounds like it might be difficult. The* schedule takes until about 12:30 when I realize that I am late to meet a couple friends for lunch. Just before I go, I see that the stock website is ready so I forward the email to Julian and Steve and run off.

And then, take a 20-minute cab ride across town (aaahhh!) and arrive late, but the lunch is fun. My friend John is getting married next week and it's his birthday today so he enjoyed being treated to lunch. The happy lunch feeling is shattered as it starts drizzling. Getting a cab is impossible, so of course, I get back to work. LATE! Darn it, I hate that. Steve is in a meeting when I return so I go through the schedule and put in approval dates (for storyboard, rough-cuts and fine cuts etc..). I also call Heather who's called – I'd missed while at lunch (figures!). She's not around. I try her cell but no answer. Darn, darn, darn!

When Julian gets back from lunch and Steve's meeting is finished, so we go back to discussing Astral stuff. We really want to figure out how we can do both, or at least be able to tell Heather ASAP if we feel we can only do one channel, somehow it isn't being easy decision. While the guys talk more about it I go back to the office and go through the numbers, the expense we'd incur per each channel and compare that with what the budget is (Oh! I forgot that I had briefly spoken with Heather in the morning and she gave us her budget range, so at least we have that). Doing one channel we'd cover cost and break even after all the studio expenses are taken into account. Doing two channels might allow for some profit but it also means buying extra workstations and finding room for extra people to work – which again eats into the budget substantially.

I let Steve and Julian know I've done the budgeting, and before they come in, I email Paul, the Aftereffects guy we'd like to hire for this. He's working elsewhere now and I want to know when he could be free. I also get a message from a designer that dropped off a CD with his work last week. I looked at it and there was some nice work, but Julian and Steve haven't had a chance to check it. I must remember to show them tomorrow. I also have a few resumes that have come in to look at – this is the stuff that fall to the wayside when it's busy. Paula has been checking the Head Gear general email and clearing that out thank God. I promise myself that I'll get the guys to check out this designers work. I also have someone stopping in to drop off an Aftereffects reel this week – he was recommended by a guy that works in our building.

Kyle pops in to tell me that a computer place in the city is selling G4s, last years models, at a really great price that we should consider. Everyone thinks it's a good idea since we definitely need to replace some of the workstations (and get new ones as I mentioned). Kyle also mentions about 10 other useful things we should do buy and check out for the move or as we upgrade and my brain is overloaded and feels, a little overwhelmed with information. I ask him if I can through it all again, when I can concentrate on just that stuff. I also remember that Steve's computer is dead and needs to be sent for repair. Well, I'll have to deal with that tomorrow as well.

Last minute I remember to email Sharon and Manny to see if the Sesame Street VHS for the Nick pitch has arrived and if it is appropriate for their presentation. She gets back to me quickly. Apparently, all is good. OK. I have to leave; I have a 7pm appointment. Oh yeah...Steve, Julian and I decide we need to meet with Heather and Fillip to have creative discussion about Channel 1, and I leave a last minute message on her cel. She actually gets it and calls back to say she'll call first thing and see when she can fit us into the schedule. So that's lucky. Then I have to leave...

## LESSONS/PROBLEMS

Deep Breathe. Deep Breathe. I'm not actually stressed as much as trying to make sure I've remembered all the little things that seem to need organizing or following up on. I keep adding to my list in my notebook, but it keeps flowing over into the next day. At least it's all written down. It's always worth the 2 seconds to make a note of what needs to be done because at least then I know if I don't get to something, it won't completely elude me.

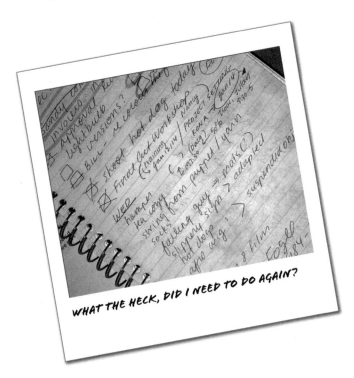

WHAT THE HECK, DID I NEED TO DO AGAIN?

## *PREDICTIONS*

- Check out more stock footage.
- Meet with Heather and Fillip.
- Buy a couple more computers.
- Budget for Astral.
- Hopefully have time to call Ashley at the Cartoon Network to check in.
- Eat cake.

## *DIARY*

OK. I get in and check email. I try to go over some schedule stuff for Astral, but get interrupted when Heather calls to see if we can go over to Astral to meet for 11:30. We spend the remaining time talking about ideas for the two channels and deciding what we are actually going to discuss at the meeting (since we are a little stumped on how to approach the Channel 1 stuff). I sit and listen and contact a couple more people about stills. Then I call Carbon Computing where we want to buy the new computers. I have to leave a message, apparently, they call you back within 4 hours. I am a little doubtful, but we'll see! Suddenly it is time to grab a cab and head over. This time, it's Julian, Steve Isaac and I.

*We get there, congratulating ourselves on our promptness only to discover that a fire alarm has evacuated the building (a test). After some sleuthing (more commonly known as looking around aimlessly), we find Melissa (who works with Heather) and a big group of people at a nearby park. Melissa then takes us over to the Druxy's restaurant nearby where Heather and Fillip are waiting (at the secret location – as I write this it sounds like The Amazing Race).*

*Anyway – the bonus is that not only do we have a great meeting and we even have smoked meat! I think that creatively things are cleared up, the concept for Channel 1 has been broadened to allow more than people to be featured (we can use objects and locations a bit more in the foreground). Therefore, that is helpful, and Heather and Fillip really likes Julian's idea for Mfun, which he and Steve pitch almost too quickly. That is excellent. The best news is that the delivery is actually better than we anticipate. We thought the major elements were due in January, but it is the packaging stuff like promos and end-pages that are needed in January. We can deliver everything else in February or early March. What a huge difference! I'm still not sure what all the packaging elements are, I find that I am unable to hear some of the conversation as the cash register is ringing every 10 seconds right behind me.*

*We get back about 1:30, Paula is off at Yoga but she left some boards on my desk for a cel job. Tourism Nova Scotia spots that need end tags done in cell animation. They're due November 6 though – so not much time to do them. I haven't even had a chance to talk to Steve or Julian. OK – there are 1 million papers and binders on my desk. It's stressing me out – must organize and clean up desk. Also must get rid of all the stuff (magazines, menus for restaurants, tapes, rubber balls) that people just leave on the corner of the desk and they have started to grow. I feel much better after doing this, and low and behold, the guy from the computer store calls me. I tell him what we're looking*

HOME SWEET HOME-MY DESK

*for and he faxes me a quote within the half hour. This is almost, too good to be true. Now my guys in the office just have to figure out if we want to get two or three new workstations (taking into account we want to have an editing machine with Final Cut Pro).*

*I also quickly do a check for the accountant's invoice and approve billing on our last Mag North visit (Cartoon colour correct and edit) and then I eat some Smarties. After the Smarties, I think I will try and redo the Astral schedule with all the new info we have. We must get them a budget. Oh yes – I have to call back an animator who dropped off a reel and I call the courier to pick up Paula's cake.*

*What is going on with the Cartoon Network? I have been so distracted with everything else that I just assumed it's going well. Rule number one: never assume. Let me go take a look. No, I can wait a minute, there's too much going on around the computers. Drew has finished all the animation so at least that's out of the way.*

*And suddenly it is cake time. Where we all sit around the table and eat our beloved lemon parfait cake and Paula reminisces about being 32 and shooting her first feature (yes – Paula is on the road to fame and fortune). For now, she settles for lemon parfait cake. Really, who can call it settling?*

*Steve asks me to call a cell animator who Julian and Steve know to see if he will be available to do this Nova Scotia Tourism job. I am able to get a hold of him right away and he's free, so now just to send a quote and see what happens. I also call to get another quote from the computer store – we're trying to see how much of a discount we can get if we purchase an extra machine and our monitors there. Tomorrow I'll look into seeing how much it'll cost to set up the editing computer and software.*

*We also manage to post a couple bumpers for the Cartoon Network, so I call Ashley to look at it for tomorrow. Now everyone is gone and I am alone – the echo of my typing resounding in the empty office. Well, it will be if I were typing a label on our godforsaken typewriter. With that – I'm off.*

### LESSONS/PROBLEMS

*That was a crazy insane day. But kind of fun, the meeting with Heather and Fillip went well – it's always better to meet face to face than have a conference cal, though not always possible. I love that the Cartoon Network stuff was going along great on*

*its own even though I didn't have much time to check on it*
*– everyone here is so great about keeping on schedule. I love it.*

## PREDICTIONS

· *Budget to Heather.*
· *Rough "work back" schedule for Astral jobs.*
· *Get computer quotes and possibly order.*
· *Call about getting Final Cut Pro hooked up.*
· *Quote on cell animation job (Nova Scotia Tourism).*

## DIARY

*I arrive to find it quite chilly in the office – why does the heat fluctuate so? Anyway, Steve and I decide on a price for the Nova Scotia cel animation job and I email David the producer with our quote. We also figure out a price to give to Heather, although she just emailed to say she's in meetings all day. She has asked for some revisions for the Moviepix logo (a previous job), and promises to send a tape with some bumper/ packaging examples from other Astral channels. This will help us get an idea of the kind of materials they expect us to deliver.*

*I take a minute to speak with a woman who does stock footage research based on an hourly rate. She has extensive knowledge of the different stock footage houses, which might be useful if we need to locate environments and/or images of people. It looks like we may end up shooting the people ourselves on green-screen. Steve knows a photographer who he called yesterday. Apparently, he shoots awesome photos and is coming in today to talk about the project. 2:30 I believe.*

*Looks like the Cartoon Network stuff is still on track – all the shots have been started and I think we're looking pretty good for delivery next Wednesday. Ashley looks at the bumper and the still we posted. One of the bumpers involves Eustace looking through a peephole. He sees the Zombie ringing the doorbell – and we're going to put a fisheye effect on it – which is how we posted it on the website. Her only concern is that they also get the shot elements WITHOUT the effect, for ease of comping in the TV screen on the Zombie head. That's not a problem for us to do.*

*Just before lunch Kyle comes into my office and we start going through all the items we need to buy to go with our new workstations, and discussing upgrading to the 10.2 version on our Macs and what that would mean, if we upgrade everything etc... It comes down to a lot of money. Having the workstations will be great but then you have to factor in the upgrades and software purchases and it all adds up. We are just starting to discuss the system requirements for the non-linear editing when Julian, Isaac and Drew arrive with lunch. We spend lunch*

---

ONE OF THE ZOMBIE'S WE BUILT FOR THE CARTOON NETWORK.

*watching the Astral tapes (the air check tapes) which have been sent over for us to see samples of their bumpers etc.. They also contain some good programming since they're just blocks of airtime that have been recorded. Saw a good Casper the Friendly Ghost episode.*

*After lunch, we all end up going back to the equipment/ software conversation. Kyle and I bring Steve and Julian up to speed on what had started discussing before lunch. I also get* the repair quote back from the Epson place, and it is about $300 bucks to fix the printer. We now can't decide if we should fix it or just pay the extra money and get a new one. Apparently, this printer may not be compatible with version 10 either.

I still have to call Tom Third, the composer we like to work with for a quote to do the music for Astral. Steve wants to say "Hi" so says he'll call, but he and Julian are in a meeting with the photographer, Sandy, at the moment and it's already 3:15. I'd love to get a quote by end of day but it's probably not doable. We may just factor in some money and deal with that later.

I keep pulling up the schedule to do a new one but never actually get around to starting. We finally sit down to redo some budget numbers for Astral AGAIN, and actually come up with a final price, so I'll call Heather with that on Monday. I also don't have a chance to follow up on the Nova Scotia quote. I'll do that Monday too. For now – I am going home for the weekend!

## LESSONS/PROBLEMS

It's amazing how you can mean to do something, which is a top priority, and never get to it. I mean, we have finally decided on an Astral budget but we've been meaning to do that all *week. Even the computer stuff – we only ever seem to get halfway through a conversation about it. Oh well, sometimes you just have to deal with the most immediate things first and wait for you "budget" or "computer" order to become the most immediate thing...*

DREW'S DESK COVERED WITH A SMORGASBORD
OF PROPS AND TOOLS.

Day 15 | **OCTOBER 21**

## PREDICTIONS

· Submit final astral quote to Heather.
· Finish a work back schedule.
· Order computers.
· Finish MoviePix logo fix.

## DIARY

Monday…Monday. I'm not feeling that great. I don't know
what it is – I feel like I can't concentrate very well. Maybe

*this'll wear off as the day goes on. We get a call from Sandy*
*– the photographer who Steve and Julian are talking to about*
*shooting stuff for Channel 1. He's going to send over a portfolio*
*for us to look at. We can call his agent when we figure out*
*exactly what we need from him.*

*We get an approval from Heather on the MoviePix fix, so*
*Isaac has put it on the Accom so we can pull it onto Dbeta*
*downstairs in the taproom. I've left a message to see when*
*they'd be free to do that. Steve, Julian, Isaac and Drew are*
*talking about Channel 2, thinking about how they want to*
*approach it and how many bumpers and so on we can do,*
*keeping in mind we have to double all our deliverables to also*
*account for the French channel.*

*The Cartoon Network stuff seems to be going well, Kyle is*
*making a list of what needs to be rendered and what needs to*
*be approved. We'll probably go over that together a bit later. I*
*just called David the Nova Scotia Tourism guy. He got our quote*
*– but apparently the project may be delayed a month or even*
*until the Spring. Ok. Just as I hang up, Bill(cell animator) calls*
*to see what is going on. So – I explain the situation to him – as*
*vaguely as it was explained to me, but maybe it'll come back.*

I also put in a call to the guy at Carbon Computing. Where is our quote? I wonder. I have to leave a message. Kyle and I sit down to go through the Cartoon Network deliverables. Everything is done and being rendered. Then Steve will take a look at it for final approvals or revisions. I keep meaning to get to this schedule for Astral – it is a bit intimidating to figure out – maybe I'm avoiding it. Or – there are too many questions. Or, perhaps it's a bit of both. I'll send out a FedEx and then do it. We got a call from Grey Advertising in NY asking for a reel, they like the IKEA spot and are working on a Pringles commercial. That's all the info I can get thus far.

I decide to microwave my lunch and then do the schedule. I've figured out that we can deliver everything with sound by mid-February, which is what we'd hoped. I just haven't figured out when we deliver the French versioning. We basically have to deliver everything twice – for English and French. I am thinking we have one person devoted to adjusting everything to French after we deliver the English. I'll see what Steve and Julian think. At least I have some dates roughed in. And with that – I need to get out of the building – it's getting chilly outside – I think only 8 C – thank goodness, I have my hat. Too bad the wool is so itchy.

I get back and realize that it is almost 4 pm. I have to leave at 5 today to make a meeting so I have to still wrangle the guys and get an agreement on how many bumpers we can deliver so I can send Heather the budget. I also have to get the MoviePix stuff on tape. I haven't been able to access it because Kyle is rendering to the Accom. I finally get an agreement on bumper numbers at 4:45 and I put together a budget to send to Heather. I'll email her the numbers first, see if she's OK with them and then send her an official quote. Now – I must leave!

## LESSONS/PROBLEMS

Even though I had to leave at 5pm, I was late because of course a phone call happened and I needed to check on everything and that is sometimes frustrating. It seems like even when I think I'm done, there's some little thing to deal with.

## PREDICTIONS

· Decide on where we're going to buy our new computers.
· Make sure Cartoon Network gets on Tape.
· Deliver Moviepix to Heather.
· Get a budget approved for Astral new job.
· Where the heck are we going for dinner Tuesday?

## DIARY

Email check. Heather emailed back to say, "Thanks for the Moviepix thing," but no word on the quote – what's it all mean? I guess she's running the numbers through her budget. Steve and Julian are working on designs – we have a meeting with Heather tomorrow at 4 pm to show her where we are with their stuff. I also email Ashley to see if we were supposed to get tapes from her yesterday at FedEx (final Halloween stuff for us to see!). She calls me to say she tracked them and once again, they were re-routed to somewhere else in Canada...hmmm. We should get them by noon apparently. Of course, we get no real remorse on the FedEx people's part. I would hate to work in Customer Service there.

We get a couple good resumes for Aftereffects people so I file them right away before they get lost, and Paula and I email

Robin to see how she's doing with the bookkeeping at home. Apparently, it all seems to be working out, she's paid all the bills and is preparing the monthly reports. Go Robin! I check with Kyle about the status of the Cartoon Network deliverables. He's just rendering the changes Steve asked for to the Accom, and hopefully we'll be able to have everything on tape tonight (do I use the word "hopefully" in every sentence? Suddenly, there is an "oh...oh" from the back room. Isaac has accidentally rendered the MoviePix fix over some of the Cartoon network stuff – SEE! This is why I use HOPEFULLY a lot, because stuff like this happens. And we still haven't gotten the package from Ashley.

After lunch, a compositor guy, Ramon, drops by. He's looking for some post work so talks to Steve and Steve shows him what we're doing for Cine Lounge. We'll definitely need post people, especially with Kyle leaving so it's nice to know they're out there. I decide to get the FedEx, the tape labels and log ready for tomorrow, so when we get back from the color correct, it'll be ready to go. I can't believe this is our last delivery – it seems so impossible.

Ashley calls to see if we have received the package. She is still tracking it. But the good news is that the MoviePix Master is getting done. That is a relief – I just want to get it out of here and not have to worry about it. And the last few cartoon elements are being rendered out now too. Yippee. Time for a Starbucks run...of course it starts raining as Isaac and I carry back 7 drinks and two cinnamon buns. When we get back, the long forsaken tapes have arrived.

We also get a call about a cel animation job so Paula is putting together a quick cel reel to send out to the production company. Steve has approved all the Cartoon Network stuff, so I'm just waiting for the Dbeta to be free so we can dump everything onto it. It's been a fairly slow day for me – which is nice since I've been so tired lately. I've been having meetings about some of my own projects over the last few evenings and it's been tiring. In addition, we are trying to figure out contracts (for my own work) always stresses me out a bit, since in the writing world I've not had much experience doing it.

So – there we go, Cartoon Network and Movie Pix on tape – and me barely lifting a finger – what a delightful day!

## LESSONS/PROBLEMS

I think all I can say is that I'm always so impressed when we have crazy deadlines like we did for Cartoon Network, that *suddenly we're almost done. It was a really big collaboration and we had to bring in a lot of people and they worked really long hours but it got done and everyone's happy. It's especially fantastic to have great clients like Ashley who really stepped back and trusted us, knowing that there wasn't time to fiddle or redo anything. That was a huge help.*

## PREDICTIONS

- 11 am color correct.
- 4 pm presentation to Astral (Heather and Fillip).
- More discussions about the computer purchases.

## DIARY

Terrible start to the morning. I get in late because the man who is replacing the back door in our apartment suddenly shows up just as I am leaving so that makes me delayed. Of course, no one is answering the phone at work and so when I show up they have already started the computer meeting, which I am supposed to be attending. Anyway, I sit in and we talk for about 45 minutes looking at different quotes and deciding what kind of system we needed. Do we expand our switcher to allow us to patch out different machine (VHS, BETAS, ACCOM) with the press of a button instead of having to rewire all the time. Do we get a digital video card or one that can handle analog too...we are leaning towards the dual card but it's much more expensive.

I leave before the discussion ends and go over to Mag North with our tapes. Steve stays behind to keep discussing the purchases. He'll come by for a final look – we just have to match to the last tape. All goes well, other than Steve having a crazy bike accident on the way over, but he's OK. A big bruise and bump on the knee. We finish and Steve leaves. I end up waiting 45 minutes for a seven-minute dub. Oh well, I read some magazines.

I get back and grab some food while putting together the tape log and closing up the FedEx package. There aren't many phone calls today or emails. Well, we get one from Heather and she approves our budget, which is great. I prepare an official quote and a first invoice for a third of the payment. I then pop over to FedEx to drop off the package.

When I get back, it is almost three. Julian's birthday is on Saturday, so we have gotten a cake today. He's leaving tomorrow for New York. We actually get him into the boardroom and sing Happy Birthday and then the festivities abruptly ends as everyone goes back to finishing the QuickTime's to show Heather and Fillip. But, the cake is saved for later. Heather and Fillip end up arrlving a bit early, so I sit and chat with them until Steve and Julian are ready. I have to give Heather the quote and the MoviePix master anyway. Finally, we get down to talking about our designs for the new channels. Overall, it is a great meeting – about an hour long and everyone seems to agree on the direction to go in, even though there's still a lot of design that remains to be done. We get good feedback about colour and branding the channel, keeping it in the Astral family. Just good points to keep in mind as to what they like or don't like so much. We have to print out the boards for Heather's presentation Monday, but the other things (like end pages and packaging details) we can keep working on and not have to make any big decisions yet.

When Heather leaves, we pull out the cake of course. It is quite delicious – 3 layers of mousse. I beg everyone to come up with a restaurant for our Tuesday dinner – and finally after many suggestions, followed by scowls at the suggestions, we make a decision; the name of eludes me at the moment. We then end up having more discussion about revamping all our tech stuff, which to be honest is just too much for my brain to absorb. I need a pen and paper and maybe even a flow chart to track everything. I also am so tired today from a bad night's sleep, and not processing all this stuff well. Maybe I wasn't expecting to re-discuss it just when I need to go home. I mean, it is fine, I guess I am just ready to go home and it is information overload. Kyle said he's come in the next day and we can deal with it then. Just one of those days, I guess.

## LESSONS/PROBLEMS

*I guess some days you feel grumpier than others do.*

ROWS OF FINAL DBETA MASTERS OF OUR
COMPLETED WORK.

## PREDICTIONS

· Get Astral presentation approved.
· Call Ashley to make sure she got our tape.
· Payroll and pay bills day.

## DIARY

This day is a bit all over the place. I'm feeling like I'm getting sick – sore throat and all – maybe that's why I've been tired and grumpy all week. We are posting Astral storyboards on the website around 11 so they can take a look and make comments. Meanwhile, I assemble all the bills I have waiting to be paid. Most of the stuff is remaining from Cartoon Network but there are a few from YTV – so better do those ASAP. I start doing payroll first, and am still waiting to get Drew and Isaac and Kyle's invoice.

I also give Ashley a call to make sure she got the tape – which she has. She loves it, and she loves the T-shirts we sent. I snuck them into the FedEx box. She asks if I could send another one for Chris, the compositor, so Paula and I decide we should send a bunch more – we have great T-shirts I must say. I wear mine all the time because it's a cool "girly T" size and not some huge

*XL men's thing. Basically, I just like wearing tight tops as much as possible (just kidding!)*

*We start posting Astral stuff at the appropriate time but don't really finish until about 12:30 or so. Melissa from Astral calls saying that they need a more specific quote with delivery dates on it. No problem, I can do that – I'm just not sure about committing to delivery dates before we really know how we're approaching everything. Anyway – I put it together and then call to ask about the dates. I also get an email with a schedule for everything from Heather. Some of the dates we discuss are pushed back to earlier deliveries. Definitely need to clear that up.*

*On the tech talk side of things, I believe we decide what hardware and software we need, and I may be able to start putting the order in tomorrow – which means Kyle might be able to start upgrading next week. We also have a bit of talk about how to reorganize the space when we move upstairs. This is re-discussed at least twice a day. I also got Kyle and Isaacs invoices and wrote their checks – unfortunately for them Steve had already left (and Julian left earlier for NY) so they couldn't get signed. Hmm, and I still haven't had time to work on the bills.*

Earlier today, Isaac handed me all the print outs for Heather and Fillip, but when Steve took a look at them he had some changes in mind. We are also posting a QuickTime of one of the rough animations we cut together so Heather can present that. That is about what has happened today. Not so much hustle and bustle, lots of talking and working.

## LESSONS/PROBLEMS

Summary…hmmm…seemed like a pretty ordinary day. I guess I find the tech decisions and computer ordering a bit of a drain. It's a big decision and I'm not that savvy to exactly what we need once we get down to the details, so it's hard to try and figure it out but still be doing everything else at the same time. That's when I wish there was only one thing to deal with a day – or even for a couple hours.

## *PREDICTIONS*

· *Send presentation materials to Heather.*
· *Maybe put in the computer order.*

## *DIARY*

*I think today may be a slow one. We just have to get the final printed boards for Channel 1 and 2 to Heather and that's about the urgent stuff. My only call this morning is from my friend Jon seeing if I can go out for lunch.*

*I do also talk to Heather to clarify the information about delivery dates. I then fax Melissa a copy of our detailed budget for her approval.*

*Steve, Paula, Drew and I walk around the space for a while trying to figure out how to rearrange everything. Should Paula and I have our offices moved up front? Maybe there isn't room. Right now, we're in the back and so anyone coming in has to meander back here since we serve as reception. We figure we could put a mini-reception/waiting area up front, but maybe Paula and I stay in the back. I already have an office so why build more walls? And Paula would get and extra wall and we'd also get new shelving for all the paper and supplies and FedEx* and crap. Most exciting, we're going to have separate and close off the tape storage area. There will be no more digging behind the rack in the pitch dark trying to find a tape, or tapes lying around with no home. Plus, now I can have a current project shelf so all tapes linked to a job remain there instead of in three places on different people's desk (or just piled up high on the corner of mine).

I go for lunch and get back just in time to courier Heather everything, she should get it in plenty of time. She calls while I am gone and asks Isaac to post both the QuickTime's we had shown them when they visited. That's done so I leave her a message confirming.

I also talk to Kyle briefly – he is getting a quote shortly for equipment, and I remind him that we're looking for a printer as well, so he says he'll check it out. Then I get pulled into a long personal conversation with my lawyer and the producer of my TV series. We're signing some final contracts and so the final discussion stuff is going on. I am on the phone much longer than I would like – in fact Steve ends up leaving in the meanwhile. I guess there's not much for him to do. Drew leaves shortly after as does Isaac. So then, it's ole Paula and I. Well, Robin comes in as well and does a bunch of work.

Kyle emails me the final quote for everything and runs me through it. I'll go over it with Steve on Monday and then take the plunge and order. I'm hoping I can talk the guy into giving us a discount though. It'll be a good deal for him, so it's worth a try.

I also get an email from Ashley with three stills from the Cartoon Network for Paula's press release. She gets back to us really fast which is really cool. I think Paula also gets her press release approved from their promo department so she can send it out Monday. After that, Paula and I chat a bit and say Aloha – time for the weekend. A relaxing day I must say.

## LESSONS/PROBLEMS

Having personal conversations with your lawyer on the phone for half an hour is not cool when you're at work. But I had to make the final approvals or Mary and I couldn't have done work on the weekend. That is the hard thing about doing your win thing aside from work – sometimes you have to deal with stuff during the day. Sigh – I just hate that. At least it was a slow day. I'm definitely getting sick – sore throat – my most hated cold symptoms.

## PREDICTIONS

- Get the outstanding bills done.
- Clear out upstairs space to get ready for the move.
- Do Robin's paycheck.

## DIARY

I think today will be my administration and organize day. There is, once again, a huge pile of bills on my desk to be paid. Paula and I are usually good at getting them done, but mainly Robin used to do it – until she had the baby. It's been a bit more sporadic. I do the usual email check. There's an email from a composer that's been keeping in touch. He's from the states and works on commercials and some films as well. He sends me a bunch of CD's of his work. They are great, we don't always do our own audio – when we do we have a local composer that we really like.

I have to first call Allan, he's our video tech guy. We need him to come in and look at our video switcher, but realize that with the shooting going on he won't be able to access anything. I reschedule the appointment. The guys are clearing the new upstairs space to prep it for the move. They really clean up the *shooting space in our original studio too. Suddenly everything looks different – neater!*

*Paula gets a call from a producer working on a Five Alive campaign. They want to do a five second claymation spot. That would be so cool! We send in a really a quote that we think is really reasonable since we really would love to get this. Apparently they want to award soon, the boards would be due in December, and the final piece in February. Drew and Steve start doing sketches to show the client.*

*In my day of organization – I go through all the resumes that have been piling up and put them in the resume binder, and email or call back whomever I haven't contacted yet. I also split the Astral job into two docket numbers – so we can track what expenses are associated with which job. I even make a new binder for each one. Amazing how the small things are so satisfying.*

*I email Dolores from YTV to see when she wants to pop by. We want to offer her some of the models or sets that we built for the shoot. I also do Robin's paycheck so she can pick it up. Then we get a package from the Cartoon Network! It's full of gifts...cool gifts too – I get a PowerPuff girls watch that lights up, and there are hats and funky metal clipboards. I call Ashley*

to thank her for all the great stuff. How nice of them! I hope we
get to work with them again – I want another watch...

## LESSONS/PROBLEMS

Why is organizing a binder so delightful sometimes? Sounds
weird I guess, but there is so much paper per job – from invoices,
to schedule to creative treatments that to just frantically keep
piling them on your desk is horrifying when you know that
any day you'll desperately need something that you used as a
napkin earlier at lunch.

## PREDICTIONS

· *Maybe we finalize the equipment list.*
· *Find out more info on Five Alive.*
· *Must do the bills, must do the bills.*

## DIARY

*Email check first thing as usual. Hmm, this routine is getting boring – maybe I should start off with something else for anyone reading this – perhaps a back walkover. Perhaps my spine will lock, thereby, ending my journal. So maybe that's not a good ides after all.*

*Back to email. Kyle's finds a discount coupon for some software – after multiple attempts to print it – and failures I give up. Something weird about printing PDF files the last while. I also get a couple forwarded emails from Paula about a new commercial that we're being offered. It's through an LA company that advertises for a lot of Japanese companies. They see the OUR HERO title sequence that Julian did and really liked it. It seems to be exactly what they're looking for; cutout multi media type bizarre stuff. We think Julian will be pretty excited about it. The money's not great and it looks as if they want us to do all the music and voice over. Still, that's two solid*

job leads in two days. Go Head Gear! Which makes me think
– maybe I should pay the bills from these old jobs! So – I make
a pile on my desk and actually sort through it and open up the
check writing software and start at it. This pile has become like
the evil pile of "to do" stuff we all have at home.

Julian gets in around noon and we tell him about the Japanese
commercial job – which he thinks is quite cool. He has picked
up lunch for all on the way in, so we eat and hear about his trip
to NY. Steve takes him through the plans we have been talking
about for the studio space. I go back to my office to keep
paying bills. Steve and Julian don't stay around long actually.
They are going over to see Sandy, the photographer, to look at
more of his photos and discuss the shoot for Channel 1.

When they leave, I call back Yoko in LA to ask for some more
details about the Japanese commercial. We presume from their
email that it is a 15-second spot, but it's actually a 30. They
also want to wait and shoot until the art director can be here
– and that isn't until Nov 19, and we're to deliver (with music)
by December 10. Many questions to answer, but we are going
to have a conference call with their creative director Friday.

The last call of the day comes from Heather at Astral.
Apparently, our Channel 2 ideas tested well and we can start

designing. She just asks that we incorporate some vignettes that have to do with the movies/cinema. Channel 1 may have a name change. Other than that the idea is approved, she just wants us to rethink the graphics – they're not thrilled with the stuff we showed them last week. We're going to have a conference call with her in the morning.

And with that, we are all going home – to then reunite for dinner. Good bye.

STEVE AND JEREMY CHOW DOWN AT A HEAD GEAR DINNER CELEBRATING COMPLETION OF THE CARTOON NETWORK JOB.

## LESSONS/PROBLEMS

*Sometimes everything happens at once. You're worried about not having work and then it comes flooding in. From the most unexpected places – apparently the Japanese commercial company found us through a keyword search on the Internet. That's funny. So much for having a rep!*

STEVE AND JULIAN, THE OWNERS OF HEAD GEAR ANIMATION.

## PREDICTIONS

- Call with Heather in the morning.
- Talk with Kyle in the afternoon.
- Get Julian to send a treatment to Yoko in LA.
- Get Printer picked up.

## DIARY

Dinner last night was really fun. And really, really delicious. There were 12 of us all together (double our normal size since we had invited freelance people that work with us also). Sadly missed was Paula who was editing her film. It was nice of Steve and Julian to get everyone together for a THANKS FOR THE HARD WORK thing. I think everyone really appreciated it.

We have a talk with Heather this morning, going over the details of last night's conversation about what we should work on design wise. She's out of town after tomorrow so we've set up a meeting with her next Monday. The guys keep meeting to discuss the two jobs, as well as everything else going on. I get back to my office and get on the phone to get Steve hooked up to some high speed Internet service at home, so he can have a home workstation.

*I also write a check to the computer place that fixed our printer so that a courier can pick it up. Once that is out of the way, I redo our 3-month calendar – and put in everyone's vacations and such. I can't believe in three months we'll be in January 2003. Yikes. Time just flies – and boy do we have a lot of work to do. I also still haven't heard from Melissa at Astral if our budget is OK. I think she's been away.*

*Dammit! I keep forgetting to mail the checks out that I did yesterday. A zillion people (including me) have been walking right in the mailbox's vicinity. And here they lie. Well, I'll just run out with them in a second. Paula is madly trying to clean up the boardroom, which seems to accumulate magazines, scraps of paper plates and any other assortment of objects as fast as you can try and tidy it. We have an interview with a woman who is a web designer and I think she does some animation as well. She shows up a bit early and is all nicely dressed in a suit. Paula and I both have hoodies on. How professional! Well, I love it I have to say – ugh – who wants to wear nylons everyday? Not me.*

*Julian just finished the creative treatment for LaForet and it's great. It's going to be very cool project – cut out style, with* mouth, nose and eyes placed on cutout cars that race each other to the La Foret store. Hope they like it.

Moments later, the La Foret people call and ask us to organize a car shoot in Japan, which will mean Julian will have to fly over there. They do want to use real cars after all. We have to discuss this because that alone will eat up the budget. They're going to present the creative concept and go from there.

We have a big "go-through" the final computer list with Kyle at the end of the day. He creates this beautiful flow-chart on his computer – anyway – we have a list of what we want – we'll order it on the morning. I can't believe it.

## LESSONS/PROBLEMS

It's pretty cool when you get a call out of the blue for a job like the La Foret thing. Even if it doesn't work out it's good to know there is interesting and original work out there. At least we're establishing a relationship.

DREW AND JASON IN FRONT OF ONE OF THE
MACS AS THEY WORK ON DISCOVERY CHANNEL

## OCTOBER 31

*I have the day off.*

## PREDICTIONS

· Lock in some sort of Astral schedule.

· Email people that I'm away next week.

· Order Waacom tablets.

· Pay our rent.

## DIARY

Paula left me a bunch of emails summing up what happened yesterday. For one thing, the La Foret job has gone to someone else, so we are all disappointed, but maybe it's for the best. It sounds like it could be an elaborate production and we're quite swamped. I mean, don't get me wrong – creatively it would have been a really cool job and hopefully we'll work with their company in the future. I'm sure it was disappointing to get that call yesterday though – it seemed like we were the only place they were bidding.

Paula also needs to set up a meeting with a guy from SHOTS, but he confirmed with her so I think that I don't need to worry about that. She's not here on Fridays so I give her a quick call just to ask about the Five Alive conference call. She hasn't spoken to Rob at Leo Burnett so I leave him a message asking if he would like to set something up. Robin isn't coming in today

– I guess the guys need her computer to do some scanning.
She'll come in next week and use my desk. I am gone next week.
Not for anything glamorous like a big trip – I'm staying in town
but have a weeks worth of meeting and seminars that have to
do with feature film development, through the National Screen
Institute program I'm in. I'm pretty excited about it though. It's
very producer oriented and in this case, I'd rather do director
oriented stuff.

Oh! The computer order went through yesterday – finally – so
we're on our way to upgrading and getting an editing suite.
We should be getting set-up next Wednesday but our software
upgrades should be in Monday, which is great. Kyle is backing
up the current computers and upgrading them to ver 10.2.
His last day with us is today. So sad for Head Gear. I have
to remember to order 2 Waacom tablets to go with the new
computers – we're going to get them at a cheaper place.

Astral update – Sandy the photographer was in this morning
talking with the guys about talent we'll need for the photos
that we're shooting for Channel 1. We may use my parents and
their cottage if they agree. I'm not sure what they'll say – they
may feel a bit shy about it. And I have to get Steve and Julian
to sit down and bang out a new version of the schedule. It's

been on the low priority list but I really would like to do it before I'm away next week.

OK – I'm going to run and eat lunch "lickety split." Meanwhile I can also write the rent check and write Steve and Julian's paychecks. I also get a hold of Ken at Carbon computing and get the Waacom tablets ordered. Hmmm, other looses ends – oh yes, I email Melissa at Astral to see if she can put our invoice through. She says she needs the original documents so I print the invoice and quote and courier it over. I also call a courier to send our reel to Leo Burnett for Rob (Five Alive guy). He just called back to say he'll contact Paula to set up a meeting Monday, but wants to show our stuff to the creative team. Somehow, these few things end up taking a couple of hours! Sheesh.

Just after 3, I go out to get some snacks for Head Gear – shopping for candy and sweets – I can handle that. Even on crazy ugly first blizzard of the year day. Where's the fluffy white snow you're supposed to get for a first snowfall? I get back and we all enjoy some pie and gummy bears and chocolate. Then I pull the Astral schedule and we rough some stuff in on that. That takes about an hour – the guys are still deciding how to approach stuff so it's hard to really finalize.

At the end of the day and we have Kyle sit down with us and tell us how the heck we'll survive without him and what software we still need and a million things like what to do if the Internet goes down or a drive explodes. Everyone secretly panics. I am going to email Paula some stuff to remember for next week – like check in with Nick Jr., set up and interview with an Aftereffects guy we like and some info about casting for Channel 1. Then I am free to go. I think.

I am gone for the entire week. You know going on vacation is exciting but also stressful on that last day at 5pm. Not that this place can't survive without me, it'll be totally fine – you just want to make it as easy as possible.

## LESSONS/PROBLEMS

Why does my time off always conflict with busy planning periods? Murphy's law. We have to plan the Channel 1 and 2 shoots next week. Paula can totally handle it. If there's one thing I've realized over the years is that people can always get by if you go on vacation. Which is a GOOD thing – because you should always make time for vacation – I'm serious, I know people that never do, and they should?

# NOVEMBER 4-8

*ON VACATION.*

## PREDICTIONS

· Driving up to the cottage for Channel 1 photoshoot.

· We'll be late to meet Paula's mom.

· My mom will make lunch.

## DIARY

Today is an interesting "out of the office" day. Julian picks me up about 8:30. We are driving up to my parent's cottage to take some pictures of them for the Channel 1 project. We are in need of people over 40 in a leisurely environment. We get there about 11 am. We are talking to Paula at the office during the ride while trying to coordinate a conference call with an agency in the States for a Discovery Channel job. We agree to call them at 11:30.

Sadly, the weather isn't co-operating, it is quite grey out, which is too bad, and it would have been beautiful for backgrounds to have the sun in the fall leaves. Sandy gets there just after us with MaryAnn (he's the photographer and MaryAnn is his assistant.) They look around the place while Julian and I call the Discovery folks. Halle is the producer and Dotsy is the Art Director at the Agency. The call is frustrating because we have to sit in the dining room using the two cottage phones and it is almost impossible to hear the people on their end. We have a good chat and the project is interesting, but the deadline is MADNESS: November 25 for two 15-second spots, and Dec 2 for the other two 10-seconds! Meanwhile we're also doing these two Astral channels and possibly the Five Alive Tag. We agree to let them know a price and if we can do it by the end of the day.

Then the shoot. It all goes fine but we aren't finished until 3pm, thank goodness my mom has made chili and salad (see, I knew it!). We are starving. We then drive to Paula's Mom's place. On the way, we have a zillion conversations with Paula about Discovery and with Isaac, so Julian can talk to him about Channel 1 design. We finally decide to take the Discovery job. It is a bit crazy because in these situations, you agree to it and then figure it out later. Julian and I try and do a rough schedule – but that only makes us panic! Now, I figure we can do it if we hire some extra post people. We get to Paula's Mom's place at 5:30. We were supposed to be there between 2 and 3pm. She is very gracious and allows us to get our shots, which takes about an hour.

Oh, we are also dying to hear from Steve, who is hours away from having a new baby. No baby by the end of the day, and we get back about 8:30.

## LESSONS/PROBLEMS

*Whenever you're shooting something, figure out how long it'll take and then add a few more hours. It's frustrating to have to be late and feel behind all the time. It was a nice break from the office though.*

## PREDICTIONS

· Organize shoot for Channel 2 next week.
· Organize/confirm shoots for Channel 1 this week.
· Schedule Discovery channel.

## DIARY

After being away days and out the office yesterday I feel completely overwhelmed with stuff to do. At first, I don't even know where to start. We have the CineLounge cast come in at 10 am for the next few days. We meet them and look at their wardrobe options. They are all pretty good. We have one problem with one of the couples we've casted. The man looks much older than the woman. Not really what we want for this. I end up calling for more headshots, and we get a picture of a woman who looks older named Sally. We book her to come in a 6pm. We are also expecting another woman at 6pm – for Wednesday's shoot.

After the meetings, I have to figure out what post people we have available. I get Julian to watch Sasha's reel (Steve and I had met with him before and his stuff is good). Julian likes it too, so I set up an appointment for him to come in on Thursday morning. He tells me he has just started a job for Kraft (NO!)

*but said he might be able to help us out over the next few weeks. Fingers crossed – he would really take a burden off Isaac who, is doing one of the more complicated Discovery spots, but also working on Channel 1. I also confirm that Nick and Jason can come in to work with us on these projects. Nick is able to start the next day actually, which is awesome.*

*Oh yeah, we have to find a hair/make-up person for the shoots we are doing as well. Paula is nice enough to help me and call Anna, a woman we have used before and luckily, she is free – so we book her for the week. I do a budget breakdown for Halle at Discovery channel, and I send the budget to Marcie, our rep in New York. Then I have to gather everyone for a schedule meeting on this Discovery stuff. We did a rough schedule but needed to wait for Drew to get back from London to confirm it – he being the animator on three of the spots.*

*Oh, speaking of London, Drew is here because our IKEA "Heads" spot has been nominated for Best Animation at the London International Ad Awards – AND WE WON! Pretty impressive and we're really proud.*

*I get a call from Leslie Hunter at an agency for which we did a TURTLES tag. I call her back and begin a rousing game of phone tag. Paula then tells me Sarah from BBDO is on the*

THE MODELS FOR THE IKEA "HEADS" SPOT

*phone. I have a feeling we are about to get some good news at a crazy time. I get a hold of her and she tells me that some commercials we bidded on waaaaayyy back in the spring have been approved to go. At least the first one has been approved. Awesome news, but I can't believe how everything happens all at once. Anyway – it's not for sure yet and we still have to figure out details. When it rains, it pours. I do some administrative stuff to get binders reorganized and start a new job for the Discovery project. In the back of my mind, I am trying to figure* out where we can get a horse's head and a squirrel costume for the Channel 2 shoot next week.

At 6:30ish, Sally, the replacement for the wife in our "theatre couple" arrives. She looks way younger and funkier than her photo – good for her, bad for us! I have to leave by 7pm, Julian stays to work, and the second lady shows up at 7:40pm. Luckily, she was perfect for what we need.

## LESSONS/PROBLEMS

Do you know what? I had barely a second to eat anything today (yet again) when I write it seems quite tame. This job has so many little details and phone calls that take up time that you forgot what you did. At least I feel like I'm back!

## PREDICTIONS

- Must find new "wife" for shoot on Thursday.
- must do a budget for Channel 2 shoot.
- We have a shoot at 1:00 pm at High Park.

## DIARY

OK – exciting news! Steve and his wife had a baby boy at 4:35 in the morning and everyone is doing well.

I on the other hand, have been better. I had the stomach flu all night. At least I am able to come in today. Man, am I tired. What's worse is, I look it. Julian and I decide that Sally is definitely too young and we need to cancel her. We call an agency for more pictures and guess what – our male actor has a wife who acts. Perfect. They'll make a great couple and be able to feel comfortable together. Nick started today and he'll be working on the post for Channel 2, he's going to start helping us sort and break up all the elements we need in each photo. We have to post our picks so that Heather and Fillip can choose what they want.

I also call Leslie back re: Turtles. She wants to know if the client can have the TURTLE model for their office. In our contract, we state that we keep our models (unless it's otherwise negotiated). I'll have to get back to her on that one(**we ended up giving it to them). I also call Brenda at Ogilvy in regards to a Crystal Light spot we did with them in the Spring. She had talked to Steve about doing some extra print ads and replacing the pack flavor with another one on the broadcast version. She isn't in so again, I leave a message. Finally, I do talk to her and explain what we can do for their budget. She says she'll talk to the creative team and phone back. I also have to ask Steve a couple things about this but he's busy with the new baby I'm sure.

At 12:30, Julian and I leave for Sandy's where we are meeting for the photo shoot. We grab some pizza on the way and get there just as make-up is finished. The shoot in High Park takes until about 4:30 or 5pm. We go back to the office and Drew is back! With award and real London, wine gums in hand. Yeah Drew. Immediately he gets to work and we are able to flesh out the Discovery channel schedule with him. He'll be animating over the next couple weekends for sure. I make a good copy of the schedule and fax it to Halle, with approval dates and times we'll post work. It is suddenly almost 7pm. Julian goes to a night shoot and Sandy's and I go off to an appointment. Isaac has worked like mad all day and we are able to post an animatic of WATERDROP, the most complex of the four spots.

I leave Halle a message before I took off.

## LESSONS/PROBLEMS

*Thank God, everyone here is willing to work hard, and put in effort and yet still remain a nice person – or we'd all be insane right now. Everyone is being spread really thin. It's kind of exciting though.*

PAULA AND MATT STUFF OUT CHRISTMAS CARDS!

## PREDICTIONS

· Shoot at 1 pm.
· Organize Channel 2 shoot schedule.
· Meet with Sasha (animator).
· Find costume person for squirrel suit.

## DIARY

Thursday already! Yikes. I check my email to see if Heather and Fillip have approved out Channel 2 designs. Hopefully, they'll get to it today since we need to shoot these next week! No word though. I send them the address to Sandy's where we're meeting for the shoot at 1pm.

I talk to Halle to let her know the schedule is together and I'll be faxing it this afternoon (I wanted to have everyone take a last look at it before we officially agreed to it). Halle says they are just going into a conference call with the client, but that they are all generally very pleased. I also have to ask for a 300dpi file of the globe that we will need to print to make a "coin" of their logo for one of the other spots. She says she'll look into it and get back to me.

Sasha then shows up – I haven't bothered to look at the time. We have a brief chat with him and explain the board for WaterDrop. He says he will be available the next couple of weeks from 9-2. I promise to confirm with him Friday to let him know if we will go ahead. I'm sure we'll use him, and it's a relief to know he can help out. Hmm..are all out computers ready to go. We did get two news ones (if you recall!).

Kyle pops in and tells me everything is basically installed and we just need to buy some Ethernet cables to attempt the hook-up to the network. We talk about some other tech stuff that I write down to worry about another day. Drew is running out to get food so I ask him to grab me something while I figure out what props we need for next week – quite a few! Oh yes, I call my friend Barb who's a great costume maker and she says she'll call me back if she can do it. Fingers crossed. We are going to stop at a prop place after the shoot to look at a horse's head.

Just before 1 pm, we leave for Sandy's. The actors are just finishing make-up when we get there. While Julian, Sandy and Fillip are planning their shots, and while they are shooting, I jot down how I think we can schedule the shoot next week. I think we can do it all in three days; maybe I am crazily under-estimating (as I think back to Monday). We leave about 4:30. We stop at Theatrix to check out the horse's head. No good because it's not very realistic, more of a mascot cute head.

Back at work, I pass on the Discovery notes to Isaac in regards to the animatic. They have minor issues – just to extend the logo duration off the top and make sure the transitions were natural and organic.

Around 5 pm, the two actors show up for our next shoot, the "theatre couple". They look perfect. We get them into make-up and then go to shoot just outside the building, which takes a couple hours. We are compositing in the backgrounds that we'll have to shoot separately outside the Theatres on King Street. I leave work about 7:30 and go home to eat!

## LESSONS/PROBLEMS

As busy as it is – the shoots seem to be going well and I hope Heather and Fillip are happy. I haven't really had a chance to re-look at Channel 2 or do a proper delivery schedule for Astral and that worries me. Maybe tomorrow?

JEREMEY OUR D.O.P SNACKS ON SOME
POPCORN BETWEEN SHOTS

Day 28 | **NOVEMBER 15**

## PREDICTIONS

- Meet with DOP and lock in Channel 2 schedule.
- Post COIN animatic on website.
- Hire Sasha.
- Cartoon Network – what props do they want?

## DIARY

The first thing I have to do is deal with our insurance. We have to sign a page with the new premium and get it back to the company – only Paula has been talking to them so I am a bit unclear on what we will be signing. I leave them a message. Then I check with the guys and we call Sasha to get him to start on Monday. Jason has also come in to start working – we are going to do the animatic for COIN with Drew. I have to call back Sarah at BBDO about the potential job but I only get her machine as well.

We have posted a bunch of our preferred picks of photos for Heather and Fillip to look at so I let them know. They are going to have a 3pm meeting about it all. Then I move onto HORSE HEAD. I get some names of prosthetic/special effects places from my friend who is a Production Manager. I never get around to phoning at that moment because Jeremy (D.O.P) just walked in so we sit down with him.

I have definitely underestimated what we can shoot in 3 days. We also have to possibly rent a bus from public transit, find a real office to shoot in, and DARN it is threatening snow next week. How are we going to be able to shoot outside?

I have to leave the meeting a bit early because I have a lunch date.

When I get back, Drew tells me we still haven't received any GLOBE/LOGO images from Discovery of a large enough file size to use for the COIN animation. It is already 2 pm and we are supposed to post this thing at 3 or we wouldn't be able to animate on the weekend without approval. That results in a bunch of back and forth conversations with Halle, who is trying to get us what we need. She ends up telling me she'd get their tech person, Tara, to call me.

In the midst of all this, Tom Third, music composer, comes in to talk about the two Astral channels and their schedules. I am in and out of that meeting because calls keep coming in. Poor Tom, he has to go and I don't know if he has all the info that he needs. I promise to email him a rough list of deliverables and dates. Don't know when I'll actually get to this.

Once Tom leaves, I call Barb to see if she will make the squirrel costume. She agrees and we decide she'll come in at 3pm on Monday to talk to us. Phew, no horse's head, but at least we have a squirrel costume.

I get a call from Rob the Five Alive producer. They liked what we posted and need a schedule and budget – like right away. Aaaaah! It's about 4pm. OK – well I'll do it between other stuff. I get the call from Tara from Discovery – they don't have what we need they're going to keep looking.

*I call Sandy the photographer to find out what his rate is to extend the rights on his photos an extra 10 years. I also need to finalize his contract. I must remember to call his manager...*

*In the middle of the Five Alive schedule, I get a call from Jeremy – oh yeah – we need to order film and equipment. Umm, could anyone have told me this 3 hours ago??? OK, fine, I get his list and put a call into PS, the rental company – seems we can get it all. I'm also able to get the stock ordered for Monday. Now it's almost 5:30 and I still haven't sent this darn budget. Julian also reminds me that he and Steve haven't received their parking checks. Don't know if I can get to those.*

*I finally fax all the Five Alive stuff about 6pm. At least Rob will get it first thing if he's already left. I then spend more time on the phone with Discovery people who don't seem to have what we need but they send us one last thing. Also, have a conference chat with Halle and their copywriter about the COIN animatic. It's approved, they ask for minor action changes, which I call Drew about and he says, are no problem. Phew!*

*I leave about 7pm – very late to meet my boyfriend at the movies. Still no sign of the COIN Globe email, I cross my fingers it'll arrive by tomorrow. I'll call Drew on Saturday.*

## LESSONS/PROBLEMS

*Why was it so busy yet it feels like so little got done? I guess some days are like that. I don't think I checked off one thing on my to-do list.*

STEVE, JULIAN, AND THE MANNEQUIN LEG
TAKE A BREAK ON SET

## PREDICTIONS

- Re-evaluate shoot due to snow.
- Call Sarah at BBDO re: job.
- Get film picked up for Test, book process and transfer.
- Hopefully do the Astral schedule.

## DIARY

First thing I have to do when I get in is write a check to the film stock company and courier it over so that they can release our test roll, which has to go to Jeremy at the rental place. Steve's in just for an accountant meeting so I fill him in everything while I do that. He has really cute video of his new baby. So, we all check out little Emmett. Steve and Julian go into the meeting with the accountant. Oh – Julian fills me in on what happened with the shoot yesterday. Due to the snow, they shot the last family inside. Julian couldn't get a hold of Heather on her cell, so they just went ahead. We'll have to wait and see the pictures to see if they'll work.

I call Sarah at BBDO to check in about the job, she is at an audio session so I call her cell. She is just getting the whole package sent over and will call back shortly. I also leave a message for Rob at Five Alive to make sure he got everything.

Isaac has posted a new WATERDROP animatic for Discovery so I call Halle to let her know. She says she'll get everyone to take a look at it. I also remember to write the parking checks for Steve and Julian, and without me seeing him, Steve slips away to go home. I really need to confirm a meeting time with him for Brenda and the guys at Ogilvy (re: Crystal light).

GETTING READY TO SHOOT THE "MANNEQUIN LEGS" FOR CHANNEL 2

I now have a few calls back and forth with Jeremy because he hasn't received the negative for the test shoot. Turns out it is at the front desk and has yet to reach him, so all is well. After that,

DREW, ONE OF OUR DIRECTORS ACTING IN OUR
CINEMA SKIT FOR CHANNEL 2

KURT IS IN CHARACTER AS THE MEAN FISH
OWNER WHO WON'T GIVE HIS PET ANY FOOD

my next calls are centered on trying and find this horse's head. Not an easy feat. I find a cool sheep head but no horse's head. Sheep today, horse tomorrow? I can only dream. Sarah calls me back and we discuss the schedule and budget for new job. More importantly, we talk about when they will need everything. They will be awarding mid-December. That job delivers end of February – like everything else. They are quoting two other companies.

After a good roti lunch, Jeremy stops by. We decide to can the shoot day tomorrow. The weather sucks. Julian and I try to wrap our heads around what to shoot and when.

I call the public transit commission about shooting on a bus but it is just a bit expensive for just one shot. We also need the steadicam but only for one shot so we aren't sure that it is worth it. Barb saves us by coming to discuss the squirrel costume. She's coming back tomorrow to show us what she finds in terms of material and all that. I hope that she'll make what we want.

Just before 4pm, the Discovery folks call to talk about Isaac's new WATERDROP animatic and the COIN animatic. I thought we had discussed the coin on Friday, but with Halle not there, we really seem to be overlapping a bit. So, there is a bit of confusion but we sort everything out and I think we're all on track. We are going to have a conference call with the client and the tech people in a little while, but in between I take a moment to call the Film Locations Library and see what they have for "offices" to shoot in. Again, I have to leave a message and I will be so surprised if someone actually calls me back.

The tech conversation is brief, we establish that we have the stuff we need and especially that we are using the right globe and so I think that will reassure the client. There is a bit of confusion after Friday's back and forth. I get off the phone, look at my desk, and there sits the film test that was supposed to have been dropped at the lab an hour ago. I just forgot about it. Luckily, the lab is 10 minutes away so I run it over.

Isaac is finishing the final submarine made of photo realistic elements so we'll post that shortly, along with the animation of COIN, which Drew finished today. I brought in my digital camera for Isaac to shoot stills with so I spend 15 minutes taking silly pictures of myself for this journal. I look tired is what I conclude. Maybe I'll put on some lipstick for Round 2...

## LESSONS/PROBLEMS

*Organizing this shoot has been stressful. We have exterior shots to do but the weather at this time of year definitely does not co-operate. I'm relieved we moved the rest of the shoot. It's good to listen to your instincts and take extra time to plan something. It may steal some post time from us, but it'll probably make the shots better giving us more time to set them up.*

PAULA (MARKETING DIRECTOR) AND ISAAC (DIRECTOR) POSE WITH THE GIANT ACORN PROP

Day 30 | *NOVEMBER 19*

## PREDICTIONS

· *Plan shoot for Channel 2.*

· *Get props Channel 2.*

· *Approvals Discovery.*

· *Go to bank and deposit check.*

# DIARY

*OK, today is going to be nutty as the last week has been. The main priority is to figure out what's going on with these three days of shooting we're supposed to be doing. I check my email and then Julian says he has time to talk about the schedule. We start making the list of props and people we'll need for all this stuff and it becomes obvious that it's crazy to shoot this week. I mean, I'm happy to try and pull off whatever we can – we've pulled off last minute stuff before but I just feel that we're spending a lot of money and shooting 35mm and it should be planned properly. Paula sits in, and she agrees, as does Julian. I suggest we just shoot the one important day of exteriors this week while we seem to have a sunny day available (tomorrow). I also develop an eye twitch, which I suspect is linked to the words "horse head". It is impossible to find a real horse head in this city. Err, a costume that is NOT a furry mascot that looks like a horse. So far, no one has had any luck. Anyway – we decide to shoot the one day.*

*I call the rental company and cut down our order to one day and then I ask for a green screen from the grip department. We're going to shoot Steve in his squirrel outfit and composite him into the live action plate. Paula and I divide all the other stuff to do. She takes on the "horse head" task and I put in a* call to Jeremy. We get some bad news, the camera test from his camera is no good, so we'll have to rent the camera from PS. That will take a big bite out of the budget!

Meanwhile, the Discovery people call. We have a conference with them, looking at the Coin final animation and at Slingshot animatic. We also talk about the final look for the submarine for Waterdrop. The final Coin animation they love – which is great. We have a back and forth about the size of the rudder and periscope on the submarine. We want to make sure it looks real and not cartoony. Discovery is entertaining, but also a serious

KATHY BUILDS THE HORSE HEAD OUT OF PAPER MACHE AND PAINT

NICK WEARING THE HORSEHEAD DURING THE NEW CHANNEL SHOOT

science channel. We finally agree on everything and we can move on with the animation.

Barb comes in with the squirrel costume while Steve is here and it's pretty hilarious. Everything fits and so she leaves. Then suddenly there are a million things to do before the shoot. We have to do a registration test on the camera, pick up the rest of the film, get insurance and book process time for the reg. test.

STEVE HANDS NICK THE POPCORN BEFORE A
TAKE FOR CHANNEL 2

Somehow it all gets done, although Paula and I are constantly
on the phone for about 2 hours.

Megan finishes the giant acorn for Steve the giant squirrel, so
we have most of our props. I order the director's chair and
pylons we'll need. We rent a van for all the equipment, which
Kurt will pick up in the morning. It is all a mad dash but by 6:
30, everything is together. Now, pray for good weather and Day
1 of Channel 2 will be full of perfect shots. Phew!

## LESSONS/PROBLEMS

*Aaaah! Why do people tell you stuff that needs to be done immediately about five minutes before that time – those last couple of hours of the day were a bit of a whirlwind. Somehow it all gets done. I'm always amazed in this industry how the impossible some how gets done. There are numerous things that need to be done for what seems like a small film and a simple film shoot.*